TWAYNE'S WORLD AUTHORS SERIES
A Survey of the World's Literature

SPAIN

Janet Pérez, Texas Tech University

EDITOR

Jaime Salom

TWAS 588

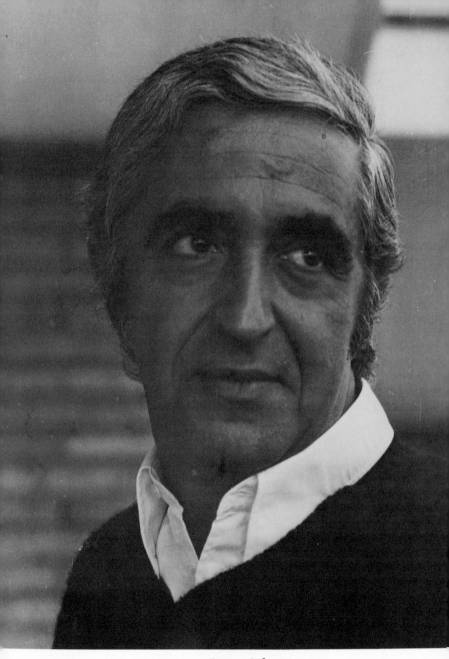

Jaime Salom

JAIME SALOM

By **PHYLLIS ZATLIN–BORING**

Rutgers University

TWAYNE PUBLISHERS
A DIVISION OF G.K. HALL & CO., BOSTON

Published in 1982 by Twayne Publishers,
A Division of G.K. Hall & Co.
All Rights Reserved

Printed on permanent/durable acid-free paper and bound
in the United States of America

First Printing

Library of Congress Cataloging in Publication Data

Zatlin-Boring, Phyllis.
Jaime Salom.

(Twayne's world authors series ; TWAS 588. Spain)
Bibliography: pp. 155–58.
Includes index.
1. Salom, Jaime, 1925–. —Criticism and interpretation.
I. Title. II. Series: Twayne's world authors series ; TWAS 588.
III. Series: Twayne's world authors series. Spain.
PQ6669.A55Z98   862'.64   81-4255
ISBN 0-8057-6430-5   AACR2

Contents

About the Author

Phyllis Zatlin-Boring holds the A.B. in Spanish and French from Rollins College (Winter Park, Florida) and the M.A. and Ph.D. in Romance languages from the University of Florida. She presently is Professor of Spanish and Chair of the Department of Spanish and Portuguese, Rutgers University (New Brunswick, New Jersey). Her primary scholarly interest is the contemporary Spanish novel and theater, and she has published articles in various journals including *Romance Notes, Modern Drama, Kentucky Romance Quarterly, Papers on Language & Literature, CLA Journal, Estreno, Comparative Literature Studies, Hispanófila, Foreign Language Annals, Luso-Brazilian Review, Anales Galdosianos, Revista de Estudios Hispánicos, Theatre Journal,* and *Crítica Hispánica.* She is coauthor of an intermediate level Spanish textbook *Lengua y lectura;* editor of student editions of Francisco Ayala's novel *El rapto,* Víctor Ruiz Iriarte's comedy *El landó de seis caballos,* and Jaime Salom's drama *La piel del limón,* and of a scholarly edition of Antonio Gala's plays *Noviembre y un poco de yerba* and *Petra Regalada;* and author of the studies *Elena Quiroga* and *Víctor Ruiz Iriarte* in the Twayne World Authors Series.

Preface

One of the most successful playwrights to emerge in the Spanish theater of the past twenty years, Dr. Jaime Salom y Vidal has the unique distinction of being the only Catalan to achieve recognition with works in Castilian on the contemporary Madrid stage. Born in Barcelona in 1925, he attended medical school in his native city and is a practicing ophthalmologist. Although he began writing plays during his student days and had his first stage production in 1955, his real theatrical career dates from 1960. In 1969 he secured his place among the best-known Spanish playwrights with the record-breaking Madrid production of *The House of the "Chivas"*, which ran for over 1,300 consecutive performances. In the 1960s and 1970s many of his plays were among the box office hits of both Barcelona and Madrid; they achieved critical acclaim as well with several important prizes, including the National Literature Prize, awards from the Royal Spanish Academy, and recognition from *The Spectator and the Critics* for the best play of the year. His works have been staged successfully throughout the Spanish-speaking world, have been made into movies and television plays, and have been translated to several languages.

A multifaceted playwright, Salom has not limited himself to a particular kind of theater but has written works ranging from light farce to serious drama. He has dealt with questions of moral responsibility and guilt, with elements of poetic fantasy, with biblical and historical themes, and with serious commentary on contemporary social problems. He has evolved over the years from religious and political conservatism to a much more liberal viewpoint; as a result, his plays reflect the progression in his own ideology against the background of a changing Spanish society. Salom has also concerned himself with theatrical techniques, sometimes revising and improving the staging of a given work as he has reached maturity in this respect. Collectively his plays thus present an interesting perspective on contemporary Spanish theater in general, not only for their diversification in subgenres and themes, but also in terms of a growing sophistication in staging techniques.

Salom, unquestionably one of the most important playwrights of his generation, will be of increasing interest to American students and scholars. Although the Catalan's theater has been the subject of several European master's theses and doctoral dissertations, the only published book-length study to date is that of the late critic Alfredo Marquerie. Marquerie's book includes only those works staged through 1972 and, because of the dramatic changes in Salom's outlook on life and life-style during the past several years, is also now outdated in its biographical information. Moreover, the Spanish critic did not attempt to analyze Salom's total theater, generally concentrating on each play individually. The present study is intended to correct these various deficiencies. An introductory chapter, drawing heavily on recent interviews and written statements of the playwright, outlines Salom's life and his evolving social and moral viewpoints. A second chapter presents a survey of his theater in chronological perspective. Subsequent chapters divide his theater according to dominant tendencies, thus providing a basis of comparison among related works. Throughout the discussion an effort is made to place his plays in the context of contemporary Spanish and world theater.

In the preparation of this study I have been fortunate in having the full and generous cooperation of Jaime Salom, who has taken time from his busy schedule as physician and playwright not only to meet with me but also to maintain an extremely helpful correspondence. He kindly made available to me much material that would otherwise have been inaccessible: manuscript copies of several early unpublished plays and of his most recent works as well as his extensive collection of play reviews and newspaper interviews. I am deeply indebted to him for his invaluable assistance with my research and sincerely appreciative of the friendly welcome he extended to my son and me during our visit to Spain.

I am grateful, as always, to Professor Janet Winecoff Pérez for her advice and encouragement throughout this project as well as in my other professional activities. My sincere thanks also to Isabel and Ramón Oliu for sharing with me their knowledge of Cataluña, and to Valerie Devar and Renee Orders for their careful and thoughtful assistance in the preparation of the manuscript.

PHYLLIS ZATLIN-BORING

Rutgers University

Chronology

1925   December 25, Jaime Salom y Vidal born in Barcelona.

1936– Spanish Civil War. Following war, prepares *bachillerato* (high
1939   school diploma) at Jesuit school.

1948   Wins Spanish University Theater prize for *Mamá sonríe* [Mama's Smiling].

1949   Receives medical degree from University of Barcelona. Collaborates in university publications and writes play reviews for *Momento*.

1952   Marriage.

1954   Birth of first child.

1955   Achieves first stage production: *El mensaje* [The Message] opens in Bilbao.

1958   Begins collaboration on film scripts.

1959   November 13, Barcelona premiere of *The Message*.

1960   December 2, *El triángulo blanco* [The White Triangle] opens in Barcelona. December 22, premiere in Madrid of *Verde esmeralda* [Emerald Green].

1961   August 8, *Culpables* [The Guilty] opens in Madrid. November 24, *La gran aventura* [The Great Adventure] premieres in Barcelona; wins City of Barcelona Critics' Prize.

1962   *El cuarto jugador* [The Fourth Player] awarded Lérida Academy prize.

1963   *Motor en marcha* [Motor Running] receives City of Barcelona prize; *Juegos de invierno* [Winter Games] awarded Isaac Fraga prize.

1964   January 2, *El baúl de los disfraces* [The Trunk of Disguises] premieres in Barcelona. January 31, *Winter Games* opens in Madrid. September 29, *The Trunk of Disguises* opens in Madrid.

1965   *The Trunk of Disguises* awarded Fastenrath prize by Royal Spanish Academy.

1967   March 23, *Cita los sábados* [Saturday Night Date] premieres in Barcelona; wins Barcelona Critics' prize. December 23, inauguration of Moratín Theater, built at Salom's expense in Barcelona.

1968   March 22, *La casa de las Chivas* [The House of the "Chivas"] opens in Barcelona.

1969   January 10, *The House of the "Chivas"* begins its record-breaking run in Madrid; wins *The Spectator and the Critics* prize. January 31, *Los delfines* [The Heirs Apparent], winner of National Literature prize, opens in Barcelona. Death of father.

1970   November 20, *La playa vacía* [The Empty Beach] premieres in Madrid. November 27, *Viaje en un trapecio* [Trip on a Trapeze] opens in Barcelona.

1971   *The House of the "Chivas"* awarded Alvarez Quintero prize by the Royal Spanish Academy.

1972   February 10, *La noche de los cien pájaros* [The Night of the Hundred Birds] premieres in Madrid. September 27, *Tiempo de espadas* [Time of Swords] opens in Madrid; awarded *The Spectator and the Critics* prize and the Bravo prize. Moratín theater converted to movie house.

1974   Establishes residence in Madrid while continuing medical practice in Barcelona. September 27, *Nueve brindis por un rey* [Nine Toasts for a King] opens in Madrid.

1976   September 10, *La piel del limón* [Lemon Peel] opens in Madrid. Begins biweekly radio program on divorce.

1977   *Lemon Peel* awarded Espinosa and Cortina prize by Royal Spanish Academy.

1978   October 6, premiere of *Historias íntimas del paraíso* [Intimate Stories of Paradise] in Madrid.

1980   September 18, *El corto vuelo del gallo* [The Rooster's Short Flight] opens in Madrid.

CHAPTER 1

From Conservative Catholic to Social Reformer

O N MAY 25, 1978, Spanish television aired *La casa de las Chivas* [The House of the "Chivas"], the play which a decade earlier had enjoyed a record-breaking run in the theaters of Madrid and had established Jaime Salom y Vidal as one of Spain's most important and successful contemporary playwrights. Salom himself, in watching the telecast, experienced a certain sense of self-awareness as he recognized in the drama's moralistic seminarian his own attitude of an earlier period: "This was I a few years ago: living life, feeling life, and thinking . . . you have to hold yourself back, because you have principles and you have to be faithful to them. And suddenly, life is much more important. The most important ethics are vital ethics, ethics that relate to life. One must learn to be a human being, to understand everything."[1]

Raised in a conservative family and educated in Catholic schools, the youthful Salom held rigid, moralistic views that only gradually softened over the years: "The long period between the explosion of my youth and the serene inquietude of my present maturity consists of a difficult and worthy effort to retrace the wrong paths, to shake off pernicious wraps, to rid myself physically and intellectually of any impediment that would prevent my thinking, feeling, acting on my own freely and honestly—like a shipwrecked person swimming against a powerful tide."[2] The evolution in Salom's social and moral values has caused him to reevaluate his own life. While as recently as 1973 Alfredo Marqueríe could write that in Salom's "middle-class childhood, surrounded by loving family, there are no complexes of loneliness, anguish, or poverty, but rather happy memories,"[3] today Salom views that same childhood from a more critical perspective.

I *Childhood and Youth*

Jaime Salom y Vidal was born on Christmas Day, 1925, in Barcelona. His father, the well-known ophthalmologist Dr. Jaime Salom Calafat, was from Mallorca and his mother, Antonia Vidal, is Catalan on both sides of her family. Salom loved and admired his father; his death in 1969 was, for the playwright, "the saddest moment in my life" (*A*, 1). Salom Calafat, the eighth of nine children born to a poor peasant family and the only one to pursue a university education, worked his way through college by clerking in a pharmacy. Salom recalls his father as a shy man who must have found it very difficult to leave his native island and go alone to the thriving industrial city. In comparing his own easy access to professional training, Salom views with pride the tremendous effort and accomplishment of his father. It was at the pharmacy where Salom Calafat met his future wife; she came there to buy medicine for her family: "They married and were happy. Just that simple and just that exceptional. I have known no other couple so close and so in love" (*A*, 2). Even now, after her years of widowhood and sorrow, Salom finds that his mother's eyes still sparkle with happiness and fulfillment.

Although Salom enjoyed the privileges of an upper middle-class home and obviously felt himself to be loved, his early years were deeply marred by the accidental death of a younger sister and by the absurd explanation he was given for her disappearance. When he was five years old, his two-year-old sister drowned. He no longer recalls who gave him the tragic news but does remember the pious lie: they had taken her to Mallorca and from there she had gone to heaven to visit their paternal grandmother. The little boy could not understand why his beloved playmate would go away without saying goodby or why his parents would send her away. "Later, but not much later, I discovered the great secret of life: children drown, things get broken, everything one day is destroyed for no apparent reason, unexpectedly and without saying goodby. . . . I suppose that that day when my sister died and left me without a playmate, leaving me alone again and an only child for several more years, the first wrinkle of old age appeared on my soul" (*A*, 3).

The second great traumatic experience of Salom's childhood was, quite understandably, the Civil War. The boy was ten years old in July, 1936, when the first news of the military uprising reached San Vicente dels Horts, a little town near Barcelona where the family often vacationed. Salom's mother and grandmother were there, but his father had gone to Barcelona to his office. The playwright recalls the anxious moments while his mother awaited word from his father as one in a long series of emotionally upsetting wartime experiences: "It was not only hunger, terror, physical and moral suffering, constant uncertainty and familiarity with death. It was something worse: the division of people who in my childhood had seemed to me peaceful and perfect into two fanatic sides that hated each other" (A, 4). The Salom house was a large one, and soon it was filled with refugees from the bombings in Barcelona. Each room housed a family, and through the sense of community that developed in the midst of the national disaster, the young boy found his own salvation from the bitterness of the conflict: "that love for one's fellowman, for the human being who suffers or is happy or simply is alive, that common denominator that unites us" (A, 5). Through his love for humanity, the wounds of the war healed, leaving, however, "an ugly scar."

Salom's early education was at a convent school, run by Teresian nuns, on the Rambla de Cataluña in Barcelona. Following the Civil War, he entered a Jesuit school on the Calle de Caspe where he prepared his *bachillerato* (high school diploma). It was during his high school years that Salom developed his lifelong interest in literature. One of his teachers, Father Ramón Cué, guided his readings, introducing him to authors who greatly impressed the young boy: Gabriel Miró, Azorín, and Juan Ramón Jiménez.[4] Salom submitted one of his class papers on the *Poem of the Cid* to a school literary contest and won first prize. At the time, Salom was not only content with the conservative religious training that he received but also accepted unquestioningly the political views of the extreme right. More recently he has repudiated the rigidity of the Catholic educational system and the general climate of the postwar years. "The postwar was hard, hermetic, cruel. We were imprisoned in an enormous cave, surrounded by fanaticism and a victory complex" (A, 5). Salom recalls that political repression and God were used as means to discourage conscience from speaking out against injustice. Among his own defects of character he lists the weight he still carries of an education and an era that he has tried to discard and that he now detests (A, 10).

Unlike his younger brother and sister, Juan and María Victoria, who prepared their degrees in philosophy and letters and who later became teachers, Salom elected to follow in his father's footsteps, entering the medical school of the University of Barcelona. It was during his university days that he became actively interested in theater. A voracious reader, he would sometimes finish as many as six plays a day. His acquaintance with playwrights included not only twentieth-century Spanish writers but also a number of important foreign authors. He took part in student productions as an actor and, when appropriate scripts were not available, he adapted them to meet the students' needs. One of his early original plays, *Mamá sonríe* [Mama's Smiling], won for Salom the 1948 Teatro Español Universitario (Spanish University Theater) prize.

In retrospect, Salom realizes that he began writing theater in the 1940s with little real preparation and with a "frightening frivolity." In spite of his extensive reading of plays, he feels that he still suffered from the "encyclopedic literary and theatrical ignorance" fostered by the teaching methods in his high school: "It was a pedagogy of names and dates . . . that avoided as much as possible our reading the authentic sources, that is, the texts" (A, 21). His real knowledge of literature came only later. "Really, it is sad to confess that, after so many years of school and so much financial sacrifice on my father's part, I am self-educated."[5] He remembers, too, that censorship prohibited him and his contemporaries from reading or seeing many works. Nevertheless, during his student days he made friends with others interested in theater and profited from their Saturday meetings.

II *Dual Professional Interests*

In 1949 Salom received his medical degree. The day after gradua- tion, at the age of twenty-three, he opened his medical practice in Barcelona. He professes a strong love for his chosen field and remains committed to it in spite of his increasing involvement over the years with theater. "I am greatly interested in the clinic, and I agree with Marañón that the chair is the most important medical instrument that I have, that chair in which the sick person sits down to talk freely about himself, to make himself understood, so that he is alleviated and consoled and, if possible, the first and most important step in his cure is taken" (A, 7). In citing Gregorio Marañón (1887–1960), essayist and physician, Salom links himself with other Spaniards who have practiced medicine in combination with a writing career. As Jaime Delgado has noted, the two careers need not be antithetical: "There has never been contradiction or conflict between medicine and litera- ture; rather one can find a number of eminent examples without leaving Spain of doctor-authors—philosophers, essayists, historians, novelists—to which one must now add the name of Salom" (Delgado, viii). This is an opinion with which the playwright would doubtless concur: "I believe that my work as a writer is helped by my experience of being in contact with sick people. In front of a doctor, many things become clear. It is not possible to lie. Medicine adds to my literary work that third dimension of sincerity and humanity that is so difficult to achieve" (Marquerie, 22). Both careers relate directly to his love for people: "My theater and my medical profession are two parts of this interest in human beings."[6]

In the first few years following the end of his university studies, the young doctor found little encouragement for his writing efforts. The difficulties in expressing himself or in having his works staged seemed insurmountable. Nevertheless, he wrote play reviews for the journal *Momento,* collaborated in various literary magazines, and continued experimenting with original plays. It was a time "filled with anxiety, fever, ardor, rewriting and tearing up manuscripts" (Marquerie, 15). Finally the play Salom calls his "authentic first work," *El mensaje* [The Message], was staged in Bilbao in 1955. In the intervening twenty-five years, Salom has continued to write almost without interruption. Initially he learned to divide his day between his two professions, writing in the morning, holding office hours in the afternoon, and performing surgery in the evening. More recently he has divided his week between the two professions, holding office hours in Barcelona three days a week and spending a four-day weekend in Madrid, the theatrical center of Spain.

Salom recalls that the beginning of his career as a playwright was a slow and discouraging one. After the production of *The Message* in Bilbao by a touring company under the direction of José Luis Alonso, Salom was to wait several more years before seeing a play on the boards again: "Only a great faith in oneself and in the work one is creating can conquer so many negative pressures" (A, 8). Not yet established as a playwright, in the late 1950s Salom became involved in the motion picture industry. He collaborated with the producer Miguel Iglesias in writing the 1958 comedy *Tu marido nos engaña* [Your Husband's Deceiving Us], a film which has been called one of Iglesias's most successful.[7] Following the staging of *The Message* in Barcelona in 1959, Salom again worked with Iglesias, preparing the film version of his own play under the title *Carta a una mujer* [Letter to a Woman]. Produced in 1961, *Letter to a Woman* was not well received.[8] In the meantime, however, the playwright's fortunes in the theater had taken a sudden upward turn. In December of 1960 *El triángulo blanco* [The White Triangle] opened in Barcelona while three weeks later *Verde esmeralda* [Emerald Green] became his first play to be staged in Madrid.

Salom had written *Emerald Green*, a mystery farce, at the suggestion of a particular company in Madrid, but it was actually produced by a different troupe.[9] By chance the manuscript, without the title page, came into the possession of the actor Ismael Merlo, who had to undertake a detectivelike investigation in order to uncover the identity of the comedy's author. A thoroughly surprised Salom received a phone call from Merlo and made the trip to Madrid to see the rehearsals and the premiere of his farce at the Alcazar theater. In August, 1961, *Culpables* [The Guilty] also opened in Madrid and gave the playwright his first real theatrical success. Salom has the "distinction of being the only Catalan to achieve major renown in the contemporary Spanish theater centered in Madrid."[10] The staging of these two plays in the capital city is therefore of special significance.

In the early 1960s, Salom continued to write plays at a rapid pace, winning various prizes, but it was not until 1964 with *El baúl de los disfraces* [The Trunk of Disguises] that he achieved real prominence. Salom calls the work his first authentically original one, "authentically mine, now free of outside influences" (A, 23). The comedy opened in the Windsor Theater of Barcelona in January and was subsequently staged in Madrid the following fall. It is the first of Salom's works to be published in Federico Carlos Sainz de Robles's annual anthology of the best Spanish plays produced each theatrical season in Madrid. As an exceptional case, the editor chose to include the work in his yearbook for 1963–1964 based on its long, successful run in Barcelona.[11] Directed by José María Loperena, the comedy also marks the beginning of an important theatrical partnership. In addition to *The Trunk of Disguises*, Loperena has to date directed seven of Salom's original plays, including several of his major works. Awarded the Fastenrath prize of the Royal Spanish Academy, *The Trunk of Disguises* has been translated to German, has been shown on Spanish television, and has been successfully staged throughout Spanish America.

Initially *The Trunk of Disguises* encouraged Salom and made him feel that the years of struggle had been justified. "At last I was at the beginning of the right road. I had needed many years not to reach it, but simply to know what it was" (A, 24). The triumph was not soon repeated, however. "In contrast with that exaggerated euphoria after such a long wait, there began the two most difficult, bitter and enlightening years of my writing career" (A, 24). Failure followed failure. "My character changed. I stopped writing, eating, and breathing, almost. I became unbearable" (A, 26). In retrospect Salom finds that he learned a great deal from his period of despair and that writers should not take too seriously either their successes or their failures.

A new turning point in Salom's career was reached thanks to the intervention of his friend Fernando Ulloa. Ulloa suggested that the playwright revise one of his failures, *Parchís Party* [Parcheesi Party]. Because the play had only four actors, it was attractive to a company using a small theater. With Ulloa's encouragement, Salom made a number of changes, added musical numbers, and saw the play, now titled *Cita los sábados* [Saturday Night Date], meet with considerable success in Barcelona in 1967. The play seemed dated when it opened in Madrid several years later, but at the time of its Barcelona production, its bright comedy was enough to keep it on the boards through hundreds of performances and "to pull its author from his depression" (A, 27).

In 1967 Salom's involvement in the theatrical world assumed a new dimension with the construction, at his own expense, of the Moratín Theater in Barcelona. Two theaters in that city, the Calderón and the Candilejas, had been torn down. In undertaking without official help the development of a new facility to replace them, the playwright embarked upon a "quixotic adventure" (Marquerie, 18). The new theater was inaugurated on December 23 with the world premiere of Valle-Inclán's *Cara de plata* [Silver Face, 1923], under the direction of Loperena. The Moratín, with 700 seats, was equipped with all of the latest technological advances. A total of seventy-two spotlights provided for even the most complicated lighting effects. The two front rows of seats could be removed to form an orchestra pit for musical productions. The theater itself was air-conditioned and had an adjacent parking lot.[12] Salom was owner and manager of the theater while Loperena served as director of the resident company. For Francisco Álvaro the construction of the Moratín "will go down in the annals of Barcelona stage history as an unheard-of and unique enterprise."[13] In recognition of Salom's contribution to the theatrical life of his native city, Joaquín Calvo-Sotelo, as president of the Sociedad General de Autores de España (Association of Spanish Authors), placed a commemorative plaque in the Moratín lobby in 1968.

The building costs of the Moratín exceeded the original estimates, but fortunately those financial difficulties were resolved by the enormous success of *The House of the "Chivas,"* which premiered in Barcelona on March 22, 1968, and began a record-breaking run of 1,343 consecutive performances when it opened at the Marquina in Madrid on January 10, 1969. The drama, which Salom does not consider one of his best, has nevertheless proved to be not only one of his own greatest triumphs but one of the most successful plays in the history of the Spanish theater. It has been made into a movie, televised, translated to German and Portuguese, turned into a novel, and awarded both the *Spectator and the Critics* prize and the Álvarez Quintero prize of the Royal Spanish Academy. In November, 1969, a second troupe staged the play in Barcelona, and in the summer of that same year the well-known actress Queta Claver appeared in it with a touring company.[14] Juan Emilio Aragonés terms the premiere of *The House of the "Chivas"* a major event in the theatrical life of Barcelona.[15]

The House of the "Chivas" was followed closely by another of Salom's major works, *Los delfines* [The Heirs Apparent]. Winner of the National Literary prize of 1969, *The Heirs Apparent* was one of the first plays to be staged by the government-subsidized national theater company established in Barcelona. The same cast created the Barcelona production at the Calderón de la Barca theater in January and the Madrid production at the Teatro Español in October. Salom's own place in the contemporary Spanish theater was at last assured. The Moratín, however, was not enjoying similar success. By 1972 Salom was forced to convert the theater into a movie house, turning it over to new management. Unlike Madrid, Barcelona has never had a thriving theatrical world and the audiences were simply not available for the sustained operation of Salom's idealistic enterprise.[16]

III   *New Directions*

For two decades following his graduation from medical school, Salom continued to hold the conservative values of his youth. His efforts to develop a theatrical career while simultaneously practicing medicine may have been somewhat exceptional, but his domestic life and the content of his writings were traditional. His dramas of the period are often moralistic, constantly repeating the messages he had learned in his early religious training. The most innovative of these plays are the works of poetic fantasy such as *The Trunk of Disguises* and *Saturday Night Date* where experimentation is seen not so much in the themes as in the staging techniques. The rigidity of his views is maintained at least through *The House of the "Chivas,"* a play which he now declares "synthesized, without my realizing it, my attitude at a certain moment in my life. . . . That kind of self-repression with respect to all of the human problems around me set me apart from them. To judge solely from an ethical position is a deformation of reality."[17]

Salom believes that the "great evolution" in his way of thinking began around 1970 and is reflected in *Tiempo de espadas* [Time of Swords, 1972], but in some ways his new concerns and social involvement are already visible in *The Heirs Apparent*, the first of his plays to contain either a political commentary or a criticism of Franco Spain. Whatever play one chooses as the turning point in Salom's career, the indisputable fact is that his approach to theater from the late 1960s to the present has been radically different from that of his earlier works. Luis María Ansón suggests that with such plays as *The House of the "Chivas"* and *La playa vacía* [The Empty Beach, 1970] Salom changed his image with certain literary cliques in Madrid, which then began to attack him. Prior to these serious dramas he had been viewed merely as a "Catalan oculist who wrote mildly successful police comedies." Now suddenly he had proved himself to be an independent playwright with his own concept of theater and with his own following among playgoers.[18] For Ansón, Salom is one of a very small group of contemporary playwrights in Spain who have created an authentic theater, avoiding the extremes both of frivolous vaudeville and of "hysterical avant-garde."[19]

If the change in Salom's theater was dramatic, the change in his life-style was no less so. The young doctor had married in 1952 and had settled into a conventional life as husband and father. His oldest child, María Antonia, was born in 1954; her birth was followed by that of three sons, Jaime, Ramiro, and Pedro. The family initially resided in Barcelona on the Calle de Balmes, moving to Farmaceútico Carbonell in 1972. The impression Marquerie gives of Salom's domestic life in his book on the playwright is one of tranquillity and happiness. The impression, however, was false. Salom's marriage for him had become outward appearance, not reality. It was, as he would later clarify in his *La piel del limón* [Lemon Peel, 1976], "like a lemon. It can be rotten on the inside but the peel always remains whole and shiny."[20] In 1962 the playwright had won a prize from the Lérida Academy for his *El cuarto jugador* [The Fourth Player], a melodramatic attack on divorce. By 1974, he had separated from his wife and established a new life for himself, dividing his time between the theatrical world of Madrid and his medical practice in Barcelona.

Since the opening of *Lemon Peel* in September, 1976, Salom has become one of the most outspoken proponents of divorce reform in Spain. The attention attracted by the play prompted the creation of a twice-weekly radio program in Madrid called *"La piel del matrimonio"* [Marriage Peel]. The show, which ran for a year in 1976–1977, featured Salom's improvised responses to questions and problems presented by the public. The playwright feels that the program dramatically revealed the "great human tragedies" that result in Spain because there is no divorce.[21] His divorce reform campaign includes speaking engagements and writing: a colloquium at Madrid's Ateneo, a special two-hour television program aired in 1978, and numerous articles on the subject. Salom's deep involvement in the issue has come for two reasons. His commitment stems not only from his personal matrimonial situation but even more so from the evolution in his attitudes in general with respect to his upbringing: "I was educated in a very rigid period in which all problems were resolved by the ultimatum, 'This is good, this is bad, and don't worry about it.'" The result, he asserts, is that for years he was "frozen like a cadaver."[22]

Lemon Peel, in addition to being an eloquent plea for divorce reform, also highlights another of Salom's social concerns: women's liberation. Salom's feminine characters have generally had strong roles and have been portrayed sympathetically throughout his theater.[23] According to the playwright, the problem of the woman in contemporary society may well be present in his works ten or fifteen years before *Lemon Peel,* but the solutions to the problem have evolved with Salom's own development. He originally approached the subject out of his respect for the freedom of others, but his understanding has grown over time: "As you go on living and studying, you come to see the tremendous trap there is for women in the contemporary world, in society, in institutions. . . . We are beginning to see a great revolution that has many antecedents, but undoubtedly now is the moment when women are really going to change society."[24] Men in general, he observes, are not as aware as women that society is, in fact, changing.

In Spain, Salom believes, men continue to have their privileges and remain unwilling to renounce their economic power. Women's liberation will undoubtedly affect the couple, marriage, society, everything. For Salom, divorce is a "poor solution," but marriage, as it exists in Spain, is a class struggle—a social, economic, and political struggle deriving from the fact that women have been denied equality of educational opportunity and earning power.[25] He has compared "that little present of marriage" with the "old servitude of feudalism by which one citizen acquires a lifelong property right on land, a road, or the water that flows from a spring."[26] It is Salom's practice to research a topic thoroughly before writing a play related to it. *Time of Swords*, a modernization of the Christ story, was preceded by three years of studying modern theological positions.[27] Similarly, in 1978, the playwright immersed himself in feminist writings from the United States and Europe as preparation for the feminist comedy *Historias íntimas del paraíso* [Intimate Stories of Paradise].

The evolution in Salom's ideology is apparent in both his religious and his political beliefs. In retrospect he feels that his view of Christ changed with his education from that of a benevolent father figure to a dehumanized ideal, to a partner in a bureaucratic structure that turned its back on human problems; Christ in His relationship to the Catholic Church had lost the element of the divine.[28] While rejecting his conservative Catholic training, he simultaneously questioned his rightist political stance, emerging from his self-evaluation as a "democrat and pluralist with strong ties to socialism." In his defense of individual freedom, he has even come to consider himself an anarchist supporting "a new anarchism in violent opposition to society, culture, alienating impositions and prejudices of any kind."[29]

Now in his fifties, Salom projects the image of a man whose attitudes and energies are amazingly youthful. It is the impression one finds in his own self-characterization: "Here I am, living, fighting, with my childlike spirit, my sincerity, my vocation, and a certain experience that has not succeeded in suppressing my artistic ingenuousness. Facing a future in which I hope to realize my best work . . ." (A, 41). His viewpoints in many respects are not those of his generation of middle-class Spaniards but rather of his children's contemporaries:

My philosophy of life and my ethical principles have changed, gradually moving from a rather ankylotic, orthodox Catholicism to a libertarian progressivism and a support of all that is implied by counterculture, human freedom and antiestablishment; sort of an acrid rejection of all that is implied by the pushing aside or domination of one group by another whether for racial, economic, technological or sexist motivation. Nevertheless, I continue to consider myself Christian, although not favoring institutionalism or absolutism. I am one of those who still believe in Christianity . . . on the condition that some day humanity will decide not to convert it into a means of domination and will put it into practice sincerely. As fortunately I am one of those who does not believe he possesses absolute truth, I must continue always seeking it.[30]

Salom's youthful energy and enthusiasm are reflected not only in his willingness to explore new ideas but also in his strenuous life-style. In the winter of 1978, at the age of fifty-two, he was persuaded to try skiing for the first time and found that he enjoyed it.[31] Not content with commuting weekly from Barcelona to Madrid, he continues to rank travel as one of his favorite pastimes.

Salom's interests and ideas have changed so radically over the past several years that few observations that could be made about him even in the early 1970s still hold true today. Exceptions are his love of travel in general and the enjoyment he derives from vacationing at the beach.[32] He has visited other European countries and has also traveled to the Far East—to Japan and Singapore. He has made several trips to the United States, spending time in New York, Philadelphia, Washington, and New Orleans.[33] He explains his motivation for traveling to be not only the facility in the modern world for transportation and communication but also his interest in humanity: "The inhabitants of other cultural zones interest me more than their monuments, and I study the latter as a reflection of the former."[34]

Salom's children are now grown. His daughter María Antonia did her university work in philosophy and letters and currently works in an art gallery in Madrid. Jaime, the oldest son, chose civil engineering as his field, while Ramiro has followed in the footsteps of his father and grandfather by studying medicine. Pedro, the youngest son, is still completing his *bachillerato*.

Given his two careers, Salom finds that he does have time to accomplish what he wants. His long weekends in Madrid are relatively peaceful ones, allowing him the necessary blocks of time for his reading and writing. The wall of his study in Madrid is lined with books that he uses in researching the subjects of his plays as well as with works of theater, many of them French translations of foreign plays. Following the disillusionment of his first marriage, Salom has found happiness with a new love who shares many of his interests and attitudes. An active feminist, she has recently completed a law degree in hopes of working to improve the status of women in Spain. While they await the implementation of divorce reform, they are quietly proving that it is possible for a Spanish couple to establish a relationship based on true equality.

CHAPTER 2

An Evolving Theater

F ROM the beginning of his writing career, Jaime Salom has ex-
perimented with form and style, avoiding to a large extent any
repetitive formula. His work is characterized by a "constant changing
of modes, styles, and genres, . . . that induces him constantly to try
new techniques" (Delgado, xviii–xix). Even beyond this experimentation, however, his theater tends to reflect radical changes in attitudes and ideology that have emerged over the three decades of his
creative work. "It is surprising," comments one interviewer, "that
the same person could have written *The House of the 'Chivas'* and
Nueve brindis por un rey [Nine Toasts for a King, 1974]."[1] As different
as these two plays may be, the contrast between some of Salom's
earliest efforts and his mature theater of the 1970s is still more
startling. He has gradually perfected his craftsmanship and developed his own approach to theater, but perhaps more significantly
he has reversed his opinions on many subjects. He affirms that this
personal transformation parallels that of Spain: "I believe that I have
evolved a great deal in this time. . . . I have embraced the country's
evolution and have changed with it. . . . I hope that everything will
continue in that direction."[2]

I Early Efforts

Salom began writing plays in the 1940s during his years in medical
school. He was eighteen when he authored his first drama but was to
wait fifteen years for his first real breakthrough: "I have always said
that one needs a miracle in order to have a play staged."[3] During
those long years of "forced silence" he created some twenty works
(Delgado, xvii). The manuscripts of most of the early plays have been
misplaced or destroyed. Salom, who now laughs at those efforts, does
not consider their disappearance a loss for anyone; he cheerfully
labels his first plays as "pretty bad."[4] Not yet sure of himself, he was
heavily influenced by other playwrights, both Spanish and foreign.

The only play in this group to attract attention at the time was *Mama's Smiling*, which won a university theater prize in 1948. Unstaged and unpublished, the manuscript copy of the drama is no longer extant. A reluctant Salom did find the original for Marquerie, who included a brief analysis of it in his book.[5] The play, written in 1947, introduced themes of adultery, guilt, and remorse that Salom was to repeat in his later theater. The title character has just died of a heart attack when the action of the play begins. Knowing that her husband Guillermo has had a long love affair with Fabiola and knowing of her own impending death, she has written letters urging that Guillermo marry Fabiola now that he is free to do so. Guillermo, however, is suddenly overcome with remorse and feels that his infidelity has somehow precipitated the death of a generous and compassionate woman whom he had failed to love and understand as he should have. Aided by his daughter, who wishes her father to remain faithful to her mother's memory, he comes to love his dead wife and to reject Fabiola. The plot is complicated by the love of Guillermo's son for Fabiola, but ultimately the young woman voluntarily goes away in order not to cause sorrow for others, and Mama's family is reunited.

Marquerie found a certain "vague and subtle" reminiscence of Benavente in *Mama's Smiling*, perhaps because of the scene of reconciliation at the end. He noted defects in Salom's style but was impressed by a relatively mature craftsmanship that reflected the fledgling playwright's extensive reading of good theater. Apparently aware of his early problems with developing natural theatrical dialogue, Salom during his apprenticeship years identified two Spanish plays in particular that he found to be excellent models for language, style, and technique: José López Rubio's *Alberto* (1949) and Joaquín Calvo-Sotelo's *La visita que no tocó el timbre* [The Visitor Who Didn't Ring the Bell, 1950]. He read and reread the first acts of these comedies many times.[6]

By 1978 Salom was able to locate only two of his first plays: *La hora gris* [The Gray Hour] and *La noche en blanco* [Sleepless Night].[7] Although he is correct in believing them to be immature works, they are interesting as an indication of the themes and techniques that attracted his attention at the time.

The Gray Hour is not dated but was written after Salom moved to the Calle de Balmes in 1952. Moralistic in tone, it was probably influenced by J. B. Priestley, a playwright who impressed Salom greatly in the 1950s. Manuel, a doctor, has discovered that he has tuberculosis. His frivolous wife Carmen is so engrossed in her busy social life that she is oblivious to his health, and even forgets that their son Miguel is coming home from school for Christmas. Manuel's illness not only brings her sharply back to reality—and to poverty—but also brings about the end of her love affair. Unknown to Manuel, Carmen is the lover of Luis, Manuel's best friend. Luis is so remorseful when Manuel becomes ill that he goes away. Ultimately, Manuel is cured. He learns of Carmen's infidelity but forgives her in a final scene of reconciliation.

The play is marred by its complicated interweaving of several subplots, including the son's romance with a neighbor's daughter, the abandonment of Manuel by all of his friends except Luis, and Luis's romance in the provinces. Salom on occasion juxtaposes young Miguel and his friends with the older generation, thus creating a comic contrast reminiscent of the comedies of manners of Víctor Ruiz Iriarte (b. 1912). In fact, in some ways the plot and characters of *The Gray Hour* seem directly related to Ruiz Iriarte's *El pobrecito embustero* [The Poor Little Liar, 1953], although the latter work is much more comical and less melodramatic. Both plots are based on marital conflicts that are resolved because of the illness or alleged illness of the husband. Both playwrights are critical of the inverted values of modern society, and particularly of the frivolous wife who does not recognize the real merit of her husband. Both misunderstood husbands are comforted when they find that they do have the admiration of a son or, in the case of the Ruiz Iriarte comedy, a nephew. Salom's Miguel, in fact, elects to follow in his father's footsteps and become a doctor.

Salom's sympathies in *The Gray Hour* undoubtedly lie with the doctor Manuel, but it is worthy of note that in his portrayal of Carmen and of Sisi, Miguel's girl friend, he introduces statements on the status of women that will form the basis of his own feminist ideology years later. Sisi protests that women do not have the right to develop an identity of their own: "We still live in a period of slavery for women. First the father and then the husband . . . always tied to some man."[8] In the second act, Carmen reveals that she has had similar feelings. She admits that she married Manuel as her only means of achieving a position in society, but she accuses him of treating her like "an object to which you have become accustomed." Significantly, when Manuel is hospitalized, Carmen is unsuccessful in finding a job and earning a living for the family. While critical of

Carmen's initial materialism and of her immoral conduct, Salom is nevertheless already aware of the economic and sociological problems facing women in postwar Spain.

Sleepless Night, which is also undated, similarly shows some influence of Priestley, particularly in its treatment of time, but features a brand of humor, sometimes deliberately illogical and sometimes macabre, that does not recur in any of Salom's published plays. Like *The Gray Hour*, the play is complicated by several subplots. The principal character is Trini, a prostitute, who finds herself sitting in a mayor's office with Ramón, a man who has come with his baby to have the child entered officially in the records. A municipal employee's wife has declared a strike, however, because the mayor has refused her husband a raise. Thus the baby cannot be registered and a body, which is later deposited in the waiting room, cannot be buried. As the long night wears on, Trini apparently dozes off and dreams a conversation with the dead man, the wealthy Pedro Ruiz. Ruiz confesses his sins to her, and she awakens with a new sense of morality that helps her resist Ramón's efforts at seducing her. In the meantime the cadaver has disappeared and a live Pedro Ruiz arrives. After convincing Trini that they have never met and that it is coincidence that she knows his deepest secrets, he leaves the mayor's office and is killed by a truck.

The moralistic tone and the supernatural anticipation of Ruiz's death both reflect Salom's debt to Priestley, but the comic first act of the play, with its odd assortment of characters and its illogical humor, is more reminiscent of a play like Miguel Mihura's *Tres sombreros de copa* [Three Top Hats, written in 1932 but not staged until 1952]. The first act of the play is so different in intent and style from the second as to destroy any structural unity. To varying degrees, all three of the early unpublished plays are marred by overly complicated plots and lack of consistency. These are defects that Salom was to overcome by the time his major plays reached the boards. Pedro Laín Entralgo is generally correct in noting that "Since he appeared as an author on the Spanish stage, Jaime Salom has never been unfaithful to the demands of decorum."[9]

II *The Beginnings of a Theatrical Career*

Salom's years of "forced silence" were interrupted briefly in 1955 when *The Message* was staged in Bilbao by José Luis Alonso. Alonso,

who was later to become a famous director but was then just beginning his career, happened on Salom's manuscript by chance and
recommended it to the actress María Jesús Valdés. The play's successful provincial tour was interrupted when Valdés decided to marry and
withdraw from the theater. Four years later, prior to its opening in
Barcelona, Salom revised the play, removing some of the defects he
had recognized based on its initial production (Marquerie, 56). Even
with the revision, Marion P. Holt has found the work to be a "moralistic suspense play of no great originality or distinction."[10] Once again
reminiscent of Priestley, *The Message* introduced a police inspector
named Ruiz who reappears with slight variations in several of Salom's
subsequent plays. Like *Mama's Smiling*, the plot revolves around
questions of marital fidelity, guilt, and remorse.[11]

The Message began its run at the small Teatro Alexis in Barcelona
on November 13, 1959. It is this production which marks the real
beginning of Salom's theatrical career. In December of the following
year, the playwright had two more openings: *The White Triangle* in
another small Barcelona theater, the Guimerá, on the second, and
Emerald Green in the Teatro Alcázar of the capital city on the twenty-
second. Both of these plays were much lighter in tone than *The
Message*, as Salom himself has noted: "My first debuts, except for *The
Message*, which was intended to have a certain emotional and even
symbolic content, were entertainment, pure and simple" (*A*, 22).
Although it was made into a movie, *The White Triangle* has remained
unpublished. In the playwright's opinion, it is "a funny work with a
third act that is inferior to the other two. One of those comedies that
an author ought to burn in order to establish his reputation" (Marquerie, 67). In spite of Salom's self-assessment, Marquerie found the
comedy to have some merit and, in fact, to have overcome the
awkward language of *Mama's Smiling*: "One of the undeniable gifts of
our author is the adaptation of language to each fictional character.
This is precisely what most humanizes them . . ." (71–72). A comedy
of manners bordering on farce, *The White Triangle* is, as Marquerie
suggests, reminiscent of the *sainetes* ("popular farces") that Salom
had been reading.

The triangle of the title is that of Felipe, his mother Rosa, and his
wife Eulalia. The action of the comedy extends over a period of time
and, as is typical of farce, is built on a series of comic reversals,
misunderstandings, and other complications. Felipe is so tied to his
domineering mother's apron strings and so unassertive that for two

years he has been unable to tell his mother that he wishes to marry Eulalia, a chorus girl. Eulalia, plotting with Chinchilla, a wealthy storekeeper who would like Felipe to establish his independence so that he in turn may court Rosa, poses as Chincilla's very respectable niece. The marriage does take place, but a year later the unhappy trio are living together with Rosa and Eulalia in constant conflict. The two women stop fighting each other and unite against Felipe, however, when they erroneously believe that he has taken a mistress. In fact, he has rented space at a woman's home in order to work in private on a carburetor that he thinks he has invented. It turns out that his invention is not original, but the couple is happily reunited. Rosa finally realizes both that the young people should have their privacy and that Chinchilla secretly loves her. Thus the various complications are resolved to the satisfaction of the four principal characters. Salom is correct in believing that the play's plot development, particularly in the third act, is defective, but compared to the earlier, unpublished works, it does indicate his increasing skill in handling dialogue and in creating comic scenes and characters.

Superior to *The White Triangle* although still of minor importance in Salom's total theater is *Emerald Green,* a mystery farce. In the 1950s parodies of detective stories were much in vogue in Spain; Salom's comedy undoubtedly reflects the influence of such playwrights as Miguel Mihura (1905–1977) and Alfonso Paso (1926–1978). *Emerald Green* is noteworthy for its careful construction, its fast-moving comic pace, and its clever dialogue. Marquerie recalls that he and Gonzalo Torrente Ballester were among the critics in Madrid who were both surprised and impressed that an unknown playwright could display such a high level of technical skill (77–78).

Salom's next play, *The Guilty,* which opened in Madrid in August, 1961, continued in the vein of the mystery play but this time as a serious, moralistic work closely related to *The Message.* Finding himself labeled on occasion as a writer of police stories, the playwright has protested that such is not the case. Either forgetting *Emerald Green* or excluding it from that classification, he has stated that *The Guilty* is the only detective work he has written "in the exact sense of the word (like Dürrenmatt, like Mihura, for example)" (*A,* 23). From his perspective of the present, Salom now believes that the mystery story which relies on a surprise ending cannot be good theater. Authentic theater, like life, should unfold logically across a series of events. Just as death is the inevitable end awaiting each person from birth, so should the end of the play be implicit, even if concealed at the beginning.[12] *The Guilty* was made into a movie in 1962 under the direction of José María Forn; both *Emerald Green* and *The Guilty* have been televised.

The Guilty enjoyed considerable success and helped establish the new playwright's reputation, but Salom had still not found the direction he wished to follow in his theater. In November, 1961, *La gran aventura* [The Great Adventure] opened at the Candilejas in Barcelona. A rather sentimental comedy of manners, it is Salom's only work to be written in Catalan. Having received no formal education in the regional language, Salom does not write it with ease and in fact prepared the script of *The Great Adventure* first in Castilian Spanish and then translated it.[13] The play revolves around a dreamer who has waited all his life for something special to happen; when his great adventure does come, it proves to be a dishonest scheme of which he is a victim. The comedy is noteworthy not only for its creation of character but also for its use of a single stage setting that provides for both exterior and interior scenes. *The Great Adventure* was awarded a prize as the best play staged in Barcelona that year, but Salom's next effort, rather than continuing in this line of comedy, was the melodramatic and overtly moralistic *El cuarto jugador* [The Fourth Player].

Holt has pointed out that Salom's early plays were undemanding entertainment and has suggested that the playwright "began to follow a policy (already established by Calvo-Sotelo, Paso, Pemán, and others) of alternating light entertainments with plays of more serious intent."[14] The playwright affirms that his shifting from one subgenre to another has not followed a plan but has been the accidental result of his experimentation. An author at a given moment may simply reflect some immediate inspiration. In the case of *The Fourth Player,* which Salom rightly considers a poor play with a totally artificial setting and has not published, the inspiration was Somerset Maugham.[15]

The Fourth Player was staged in Lérida by an amateur troupe in 1962 and was awarded a prize by that city's Royal Academy. The scene of the drama is a Protestant mission, presumably in the South Pacific. Robert, the missionary, has just returned to the island with his new bride, Carlota. She is a former Catholic who converted and then divorced Javier, her wealthy landowner husband, who still resides on the island. As the play progresses, Carlota becomes increasingly guilty about her divorce and begins to blame Robert for having caused her to give up the true faith and the Virgin Mary. When Javier appears to have attempted suicide and Carlota discovers that she is pregnant, her remorse and her rejection of Robert and his religion reach a climax. In that the Catholic Church does not recognize divorce, she considers herself still married to Javier. She writes to the bishop offering her life in exchange for Javier's. Javier recovers. Carlota dies in childbirth but arranges for Javier to raise her child as a Catholic. Except for the introduction of a flashback, a new technique for Salom, the play has little to commend itself as theater but is an interesting measure of how radically the playwright's religious and moral views have changed from the early 1960s to the present.

In 1963 Salom won two more prizes, the City of Barcelona for *Motor en marcha* [Motor Running], a play that has never been staged or published in Spain although it has been translated into German, and the Isaac Fraga prize for *Juegos de invierno* [Winter Games], which premiered in Madrid in January of the following year and was later televised. *Motor Running*, according to Salom, is interesting primarily as a thematic precursor of *The Heirs Apparent*.[16] Like the later, more successful drama, *Motor Running* deals with the conflict between father and son in their attitudes toward the family business enterprise and toward society. Victoriano, the father, is the head of a large trucking firm, which he formed years before through an apparently exploitive manipulation of his original partners. One of them, Emilio, still drives a truck for him. Luis, who joins Emilio on his route, is Victoriano's rebellious son; he is sent out as a driver in punishment for forgery. Attempting to undermine his father's company and to maintain the friendship of the domineering and dishonest Nico, Luis joins in a conspiracy to hijack Emilio's truck. He also seduces Emilio's daughter-in-law, whose own husband has gone to America alone following a dispute with Victoriano. In the meantime Victoriano's other son, Alberto, who dutifully helps his father run the business, has fallen in love with Victoriano's secretary; the father, however, wants Alberto to marry a wealthy woman and proposes to the secretary himself.

Victoriano is shown to be as exploitive of others as Luis believes, but Luis eventually comes to realize that the hijackers and he also use people for their own selfish ends. Emilio mortgages his house to send his pregnant daughter-in-law to her husband, in the hopes of saving that marriage. Alberto is killed in an auto accident, and Victoriano becomes ill and dies. Luis at first turns to alcohol as an escape but finally decides that he must shoulder the responsibility for the family business, in part for the sake of the employees. Like most of Salom's early plays, the tone of *Motor Running* is moralistic and the conclusion is one in which the principal character, chastened by a family tragedy, repents and reforms. Nevertheless, in his portrayal of Victoriano, Salom does reveal his emerging antiestablishment views. Marquerie, in his reading of *Motor Running*, felt that the most salient aspect of the play was its cinematographic technique (151–52). Salom, showing his continuing interest in theatrical innovation, uses a split stage and develops both flashbacks and simultaneous scenes. To create the impression of a moving truck, he proposes that the actors playing Emilio and Luis keep their bodies in motion when they are supposedly on the road.

Much more conventional in its staging than *Motor Running*, *Winter Games* is, in fact, an earlier work. The comedy, which takes place in an isolated old folks' home, antedates *Emerald Green*. Salom recalls that, before any of his premieres in Barcelona or Madrid, he sent *Winter Games* to a director in the capital. The play was rejected with the following comment: "I am sorry to say that I am very angry with you. Your comedy, which I've just finished reading, really pleased me. It's a marvelous comedy, both for its dialogue and its theme. But why in the devil do you write plays that are impossible to produce? Who can stage a comedy with five old men?"[17] The 1964 production was directed by Cayetano Luca de Tena, who apparently did not share the other director's reservations. Bearing some resemblance to a mystery farce, *Winter Games* nevertheless transcends light comedy in presenting with sympathy the fears of the old men who correctly believe that one of them will die before spring comes.

January, 1964, also witnessed the premiere of *El hombre del violín* [The Man with the Violin], the last of Salom's unpublished plays. A complicated work partially in the style of the *sainete* and certain comedies of manners, it was written expressly for the well-known comic actor Francisco Martínez Soria and was staged in Palma de Mallorca. The title character, don Fermín, is closely related to a repeated *pobrecito* figure in the theater of Ruiz Iriarte in the 1950s.[18] He is a modest but dignified and cultured street musician who is asked to assume the role of a French-speaking businessman in order to help Rosendo deceive his wife. Rosendo has told Marta that a Mr. Tibeau is in town as an excuse to go away with his mistress Gloria; now he must produce Mr. Tibeau in order to keep Marta from learning the truth. Don Fermín agrees to the deception in order to earn money to help his young friends Lucita and Julián buy an apartment and marry. Marta learns the truth, but nonetheless she and Rosendo are finally reconciled. Julián loses the money in a fraudulent real estate scheme, but Rosendo eventually helps the young couple. In addition to these complications, however, the plot also revolves around don Fermín's true identity and the source of his valuable violin. In this aspect and in the introduction of a kleptomaniac maid, *The Man with the Violin*, like *Emerald Green*, is a mystery farce. Salom manages to untangle the many strands of his story and to handle with some skill a split stage setting, but Marqueríe is undoubtedly correct in asserting that the play failed for its "excessive accumulation of incidents and its mixture of tones and styles" (135). Its structural weaknesses would, in fact, suggest that it was written quite some time prior to its premiere.

III *Great Triumphs and Continued Disappointments*

In January, 1964, simultaneously with the moderate success of *Winter Games* and the disappointment of *The Man with the Violin*, Salom's first major triumph, *The Trunk of Disguises*, opened in Barcelona. The playwright's experimentation with staging techniques reached a mature level in this work. A play of poetic fantasy, *The Trunk of Disguises* portrays an old man who is able during one magical evening to relive a series of amorous adventures from various periods in his life. The transitions are facilitated by the appropriate use of costume and music, resulting, as Holt has noted, in a certain intended "Music Hall" flavor.[19] All of the roles from the several time sequences are played by the same three actors. This use of doubling is one that Salom would develop with variations in his later theater. The overwhelming success of *The Trunk of Disguises* came as a surprise to the theater management, which had expected the innovative fantasy to run for a single performance and had already begun rehearsing a "more commercial work" to follow it (*A*, 23–24).

In his next play, Salom did not continue in the line of *The Trunk of Disguises* but rather reverted to his earlier moralistic dramas. *Falta de pruebas* [Lack of Evidence], which had its premiere in Barcelona in September, 1964, deals once again with adultery and guilt and, like *The Message* and *The Guilty*, uses some techniques of the detective story. Not satisfied with the play, Salom later revised it under the title *La noche de los cien pájaros* [The Night of the Hundred Birds]. The latter version, which opened in Madrid in February, 1972, was much more successful and was subsequently made into a movie. Both plays utilize a multiple stage setting, but the revised drama reduces the number of settings and characters. It also introduces a greater fluidity of time than that of the original play.

In 1965 the Catalan playwright staged two additional plays, one a work of serious, moralistic intent, and the other a light entertainment. *Espejo para dos mujeres* [Mirror for Two Women] opened in the Windsor Theater of Barcelona in September and in the Alcázar Theater of Madrid in November. It has also been shown on Spanish television. The play contrasts two sisters, one who has led a secluded and pious life in a provincial Spanish city and the other, sophisticated and no longer religious, who returns from France with her lover. Salom recalls that the play reflected the influence of Priestley's *Eden End*.[20] December marked the Madrid premiere of *Parcheesi Party*. Directed by José Osuna, this latter comedy, somewhat related in technique to *The Trunk of Disguises*, presented the imaginary love adventures of a provincial wife. The four actors in the play portray the variety of roles required by the one character's daydreams. *Parcheesi Party*, like *Mirror for Two Women* and, to a lesser extent, *Lack of Evidence*, was a failure. Thoroughly discouraged, Salom turned his attention to movies, collaborating on the script of *Muerte en primavera* [Death in the Spring].[21] The playwright returned to the stage in 1967 with a revised version of *Parcheesi Party*. Now titled *Saturday Night Date*, the comedy opened in Barcelona in March and was awarded that city's Critics' Easter Sunday prize. In rewriting the play, Salom changed some of the imaginary adventures, altered the staging technique, and added several musical numbers, thus relating it more closely to the "Music Hall" effect of *The Trunk of Disguises*.

Saturday Night Date was Salom's first real success after *The Trunk of Disguises*. Both of these comedies were works of poetic fantasy and to differing degrees could well be considered light entertainment. Completely different in tone and intent was his next triumph, the record-breaking *The House of the "Chivas"*. The action of this drama takes place in a house in the vicinity of Barcelona in the final days of the Civil War and deals in large part with the involvement of some Republican soldiers with the daughters of the family with whom they are living. In spite of the political and social background, Salom's emphasis is on religious and moral questions, thus relating the play to a main current of his previous theater. Although *The House of the*

"Chivas" was not staged until 1968, it had actually been written several years earlier, thus explaining its ideological stance. The playwright has declared that the drama represented a step backward in his thinking even in 1964 when he wrote it, but that he had felt impelled to dramatize the Civil War because of the enormous impact it had had on his childhood.[22]

The House of the "Chivas" was followed closely by another serious drama, the prize-winning *The Heirs Apparent*. The play, which opened in Barcelona in January, 1969, and was later televised, portrays three generations of an industrial family and the struggle between the capitalists and the workers. When the son and grandson are unwilling or unable to take the place of the dead patriarch, the dynasty comes to an end. On one level the play is clearly related to *Motor Running* with its conflict between father and son over the family business, but on another level the dramatic situation is symbolic of the political reality in Spain as General Francisco Franco (1892–1975) reached his declining years. Salom states that *The Heirs Apparent* is an oblique commentary on the decadence of the Franco regime but that it could also be interpreted as the decadence of any system.[23] Fellow playwright Carlos Muñiz has noted that in plays such as *The House of the "Chivas," The Heirs Apparent,* and *Lemon Peel* Salom has chosen timely themes; in the case of *The Heirs Apparent* he has even presented a "dramatic precursor of historic situations."[24]

The decade of the 1960s, which marks the beginning of Salom's successful theatrical career, represents a continued period of experimentation with mixed results. The plays written and staged during these years varied from dismal failures to the enormous triumph of *The House of the "Chivas"* and ranged in style and technique from very traditional moralistic dramas to highly innovative works of poetic fantasy. The playwright tried his hand at several subgenres, including mystery farces, comedies of manners, and melodrama. His writing, particularly in the early 1960s, reflected the strong influence of divers authors, including J. B. Priestley, Somerset Maugham, Anton Chekhov, and Spanish writers of *sainetes* and comedies. Although three of his most important or successful plays date from this period—*The Trunk of Disguises, The House of the "Chivas,"* and *The Heirs Apparent*—Salom believes that it was not until the 1970s that he reached his full maturity as a playwright.[25]

IV *The Mature Plays of the 1970s*

Salom's theater of the current decade has been more consistently of high quality than his earlier efforts but continues to display a tendency to experiment with various subgenres and styles. Quite different from *The Heirs Apparent* with its social and political themes are the two plays produced in 1970. *The Empty Beach*, which opened at the Lara in Madrid in November, is a religious allegory. *Viaje en un trapecio* [Trip on a Trapeze], which had its premiere at the Moratín in Barcelona a week later, is a work of poetic fantasy, related at least in its staging techniques to the earlier plays of light entertainment, *The Trunk of Disguises* and *Saturday Night Date*. *The Empty Beach* has been made into a movie and excerpts from it have been shown on Spanish television; *Trip on a Trapeze* has been televised but has never been staged in Madrid.

The setting for *The Empty Beach* is an isolated summer resort. It is autumn and all the tourists have left. The woman who runs the resort finds herself alone with the young man who has entertained the female guests. These two characters and two other rather mysterious figures who complete the cast have obvious symbolic values, representing life, physical pleasure, death, and God. Salom's interest in religious themes has been apparent from his earliest plays but comes to the forefront in this allegory and the later *Time of Swords*. *Trip on a Trapeze*, like the other plays of poetic fantasy, has a very small cast, with each of the actors doubling in more than one role. The background for the farce is the circus world, but, as Holt has noted, behind the superficial level of light comedy and theatricality there is a serious intent.[26] At heart, Salom's characters, who are somewhat reminiscent of the role-playing figures of Fernando Arrabal's *L'Architecte et l'empereur d'Assyrie* [The Architect and the Emperor of Assyria, 1967], are anguished human beings.

In 1971 Salom embarked on a new aspect of his theatrical career with the preparation of the Spanish version of Max Frisch's *The Chinese Wall* (1955). Staged at the Teatro de Bellas Artes in Madrid under the direction of José Tamayo, the play was well received, running for more than one hundred performances. Frisch's play is a kind of historical farce, developing simultaneously the perspectives both of the past and of the present, and relates closely to Salom's own later *Nueve brindis por un rey* [Nine Toasts for a King] as well as to a number of other contemporary Spanish works.

The following year saw the Madrid premieres of *The Night of the Hundred Birds*, the revised *Lack of Evidence*, and of *Time of Swords*, a serious play that demonstrated once again Salom's interest in religious and biblical themes. Both plays ran for more than four hundred performances. Speaking to the Círculo de Bellas Artes (Fine Arts Club) in Madrid in March, 1972, Salom indicated that he had just spent three years studying modern theological positions as preparation for his latest play. His lecture on "Radical Theology in the Theater" clearly indicated his belief that theater often has concerned itself with the relationship between God and man and that it should continue to do so.[27] *Time of Swords* itself is a modernization of the Christ story, with the twelve disciples symbolizing a variety of attitudes and ideologies present in contemporary society, but it is also a play of political commentary. Salom's research convinced him that Christ's followers began as revolutionaries opposed to a foreign invader: "After removing the clothing with which tradition, imagination, and baroque artistry had disguised the figures of the Apostles, I realized that all of them, left in flesh and blood, were integrally politicized. They expected a national liberation from Christ."[28] Salom's demythification and politicization of the disciples caused him problems with the censor, thus delaying the premiere (*A*, 34). For Ansón the play is one of denunciation that "tears away masks and holds a mirror up to the naked faces."[29] *Time of Swords* shared with Antonio Gala's *Los buenos días perdidos* [The Good Days Lost] the *Spectator and the Critics* prize for 1972.

In 1973 Salom staged no new original plays, but *Time of Swords* opened in Barcelona and *Saturday Night Date* was finally produced in the capital city, with a moderately successful run of more than one hundred performances. In this year Salom also prepared a stage version of a second foreign play, *The Hostage* (1958) by Brendan Behan. The production, directed by Loperena, opened in the Bellas Artes in Madrid on December 14. The Irish comedy met with negative reviews, but it is significant that Salom was strongly attracted to the text.[30] The play, which revolves around a political prisoner in the Irish Civil War, had earlier been labeled obscene in Spain; it includes a blend of speech, song, and dance, with a certain amount of earthy humor.

Salom's historical farce *Nine Toasts for a King* opened in Madrid on September 27, 1974, after a delay of almost a year in receiving approval from the censors. Based on the fifteenth-century Compromiso de Caspe, a meeting held to select the successor to Martín I, *el Humano*, king of Aragón, Cataluña, and Valencia, who had died without an heir, *Nine Toasts for a King*, like *The Heirs Apparent*, was intended to make an indirect commentary on the end of the Franco regime.[31] The censors apparently were more inclined to see the contemporary political message than were the critics, who judged the work rather harshly. It nevertheless enjoyed a run of more than one hundred performances. A proposal to translate the work into Catalan never materialized for political reasons although the historical theme was obviously of regional interest.[32]

Nine Toasts for a King, similar in structure to a number of other historical plays of recent years, moves in time and space with great fluidity. Like *The Trunk of Disguises* and *Saturday Night Date*, it also makes use of song. More successful both with critics and with the public, and, in many ways more innovative in its staging, is Salom's next work, *Lemon Peel*. This drama, which inaugurated the playwright's campaign for divorce reform in Spain, is of particular interest for its use of doubling. The same actress plays the roles of the main character's daughter and his mistress, thus making visible the man's internal conflict as he is torn between his new love and his genuine affection for his child. In theatrical technique *Lemon Peel* is related to the earlier plays of poetic fantasy in which Salom had also used doubling, but in its theme it is more closely aligned with the later works of political and social commentary. The play opened in the Marquina in Madrid on September 10, achieved more than five hundred performances, and was awarded the Espinosa and Cortina prize of the Royal Spanish Academy in 1977.

In 1978 Salom was at work simultaneously on two very different projects, a feminist comedy based on a biblical story and a rock musical dealing with a medieval youth crusade. *Intimate Stories of Paradise*, which opened in October in Madrid, exploits the legend of Lilith, the first partner of Adam. Unlike Eve, who was created to be subservient to man, Lilith was Adam's equal. While the playwright's sympathies are with Lilith, he found that many of the Spanish playgoers, male and female, sided with Eve.[33] The musical, tentatively entitled *Las cruzadas* [The Crusades], continues somewhat in the vein of *Time of Swords* and *Nine Toasts for a King* in its intentional demythification and modernization of history. Although the manuscript was completed before that of *Intimate Stories of Paradise*, the ambitious nature of the undertaking has necessarily delayed its staging.[34] The musical score was ready by the beginning of the 1979–80 season, but in early 1981 the musical had still not been scheduled for an opening. In the meantime, Salom has written and staged *El corto vuelo del gallo* [The Rooster's Short Flight], a polemical treatment of the life of Franco's father which opened in Madrid in September, 1980.

V   Salom's Views on Theater

If there is a constant in the theater of Jaime Salom, it is his preoccupation with human beings. He has stated, "As for the problems of the contemporary world that are worthy of being staged, I would put in first place the human condition: individual (i.e., psychological theater) or as representative, symbol, or archetype of human groups, of millions of people who are in analogous conditions and with whom all problems take on universal stature" (Marquerie, 23). He has repeatedly observed that his medical career has served him well in understanding people and in deepening his love for humanity. In this respect he has found that his two professions reinforce one another.

Beyond his avowed love for humanity, Salom also reveals a continuing love for theater itself. "Theater for me is almost a physical necessity. It does not serve me as an escape but quite the contrary: it takes control of me and envelops me" (Marquerie, 24). Consistent with his own tendency to experiment with various subgenres and techniques, he does not believe that one kind of theater is automatically superior to any other. "The great advantage of theater is that it has no rules. The secret is that it has no secrets. . . . If a play produces authentic emotion in the author, it will find an echo. The author is not alone if he says something with sincerity."[35] Theater is thus a means of expression and communication, "an intermediary between an author and some spectators—the complete understanding and appreciation of a dramatic work cannot be achieved through reading it—who are spiritually united in a way by this link" (Delgado, xx).

Salom's theater has sometimes been evaluated negatively by critics who find it too commercial. Writing in 1970, Joan de Sagarra considered Salom the top playwright in Spain but lamented that his theater was aimed at the consumer and avoided controversy.[36] Several years later, even after Salom had begun staging works with increasing emphasis on social and political themes, Perico Pomar commented that some people considered Salom "a kind of Alfonso Paso, but good."[37] Although Salom says that he has been surprised by his box office success, he is not offended that his theater is "commercial." He considers contemporary Spanish theater to be equal in quality to that of other European countries and does not believe that plays must be frivolous to attract an audience. "If by commercial you mean to fill the theater, amusing people and making them laugh, then no. I'm not commercial. If by commercial you mean to fill a theater, interesting an audience, and making them think—then yes, I am. Shakespeare and Brecht are commercial."[38] In an essay on Azorín's ideas about theater, Salom raises again the same question posed in 1927 by the earlier Spanish writer: "Is it not possible to change and ennoble the theater through the so-called commercial theater, consumer theater, the theater that fills the auditoriums of Madrid or Barcelona, just so long as the works staged are of quality and sensitivity? The master asks, is Valéry superior to Racine? Today we would say, is Kopit superior to Miller or Molière?"[39] To be of value, theater does not have to be limited to a select minority in its appeal.

In agreement with Azorín on many aspects of theater, Salom shares his views of criticism as well as his ideas on commercial theater. Azorín held in an article published in 1926 that immediately following a premiere no one knows if a drama is good or bad.[40] Salom compares the initial, emotional response to a play with the impact of learning of the death of a friend. Given the subjective nature of the experience, of the direct communication from person to person, it is impossible for the critic to analyze a play objectively as soon as the curtain falls. Critics, like other spectators, should allow themselves to be carried along by the magic, the fantasy, that is theater. Unfortunately, they have deadlines to meet and either cannot immerse themselves in the play as they should or cannot wait for the more objective evaluation that comes only with time. Sometimes, of course, particularly in postwar Spain, they have evaluated individual plays in accordance with a bias for or against a specific kind of theater. Salom rejects such an ideological approach. In evaluating theater, he subscribes to Goethe's "three golden rules": (1) What was the author's purpose in writing the play? (2) Was the goal achieved? (3) Was it worth the effort?[41] In accordance with this concept, he has singled out two very different contemporary Spanish playwrights as among those who deserve greater international attention, Antonio Buero Vallejo and Miguel Mihura.[42]

Salom's approach to theater has evolved over the years, concomitant with an unquestionable improvement in quality. He acknowledges that his earliest works were frivolous, but that he then began to

seek greater depth. "I believe that my work has become more intellectual with the passage of time. Now I am a more dialectical author, a
more testimonial one in the profound sense of the word. A richness
has resulted that was previously lacking because of inexperience.
Theater is perhaps the literary art that most needs time in order to
reach a certain maturity."[43] The many prizes his plays have won are at
least a partial indication that his self-assessment is correct. According
to some critics he is one of the three or four most important playwrights in Spain today.[44] For Salom, who was able to sustain his
writing over many years of silence and failure, positive critical opinion is probably less significant to his continued work than his own
need to create. His response several years ago to the question "What
is literary creation?" reflects both his love of theater and his personal
motivation as a playwright: "It is the revelation, by means of words, of
a new reality, of another life that can come to be more authentic and
more human than that which is actually lived."[45]

CHAPTER 3

Inspector Ruiz Calls:
Plays of Guilt and Remorse

I N THE early years of Jaime Salom's theatrical career, his plays were often labeled mysteries, a classification which he has generally rejected. Indeed, most of his plays that have some of the characteristics of the mystery drama—revelation of a crime, suspense, judgment as to the relative guilt or innocence of a particular character—do not fully belong to the category of detective story but rather are moralistic drama. They are not "whodunits" in the usual sense of the term. The question is not who committed the crime, but what motivated the person to act as he or she did and whether or not those morally responsible can assume their burden of guilt.

When Salom began having plays staged in the late 1950s and early 1960s, Spanish theater was witnessing a vogue in mystery plays, works strongly influenced by British writers such as Agatha Christie and J. B. Priestley. Sainz de Robles in his theater yearbooks reports five productions in Madrid of plays by Christie and four by Priestley during the theatrical seasons from 1949–1950 to 1959–1960.[1] Spanish plays related to the mystery subgenre fall generally into two categories. There were light comedies that functioned as parodies of detective stories; these farces are best exemplified by certain works of Paso and Mihura and also include Salom's *Emerald Green*.[2] The other group of plays, which includes most of Salom's suspense dramas, owes a greater debt to Priestley than to Christie, comprising serious works usually tending toward psychological or social drama.

Among Priestley's plays presented in Madrid in the 1950s were *Dangerous Corner* (1932), *I Have Been Here Before* (1937), and *An Inspector Calls* (1945). Although none of Salom's plays are directly imitative of these works, there are certain themes and techniques in the British plays that found an echo in the Catalan's theater along with that of other Spanish playwrights. *Dangerous Corner* and *An Inspector Calls* in particular have been of continuing interest in Spain. The former drama was produced in the 1950s under the title *Curva peligrosa*, followed in 1963 with a new version *Esquina peligrosa* and in 1973 with a third translation, *Deja dormir al perro dormido*.[3] *An Inspector Calls*, which has been labeled "the first important work of the new social theater to appear in the West after the Second World War,"[4] became known almost immediately in Spain in the 1940s under the title *La herida del tiempo*. This version, translated and directed by Luis Escobar, was staged in Madrid at the María Guerrero. A second version, presented by Cayetano Luca de Tena, was called *Llama un inspector* and was staged at the Español during the 1950–1951 season. A revival in 1972, directed by José Osuna at the Reina Victoria, ran for more than two hundred performances.[5]

Dangerous Corner has a complicated, suspenseful plot, revolving around a series of love triangles and an alleged suicide. Three couples and two of their business associates are enjoying a pleasant social evening until they begin to seek the truth behind Martin Caplan's death the year before, thus gradually tearing away each other's masks. Their mutual interrogation reveals not only that the suicide was really an accident but that the various characters have been involved in adultery, homosexuality, and theft. Robert Caplan is so disillusioned by the night's revelations that he apparently commits suicide. The conclusion of the play, however, remains ambiguous. Priestley ends the action where it began, with a radio program in which a shot is fired. In the first act, this episode is followed by the conversation that leads to the search for truth. In the last act, the same episode is followed by a different conversation, thus creating the impression of a circular time but with the possibility that the night's interrogation—and hence the second death—never took place.

Nonlinear time is also the basis of *I Have Been Here Before*. A German doctor in the play holds a theory of reincarnation in which life is a spiral; existence is repeated but with the possibility for change if we have knowledge. The action again concerns a love triangle. The young wife of an older businessman is fated to fall in love with another man, as she has always done in the past. The lovers have always run away together, leaving the husband to commit suicide and condemn the investors in his company to sudden ruin. The lovers in turn have found not happiness but poverty and misery. Because of the doctor's intervention, this time the husband understands and forgives. He allows his wife to leave him and vows that no one will suffer. Through his sacrifice, he finds spiritual peace.

An Inspector Calls, like *Dangerous Corner,* has some outward characteristics of the mystery play, but the questions it raises are of a moral and social nature that transcend the usual detective story. A mysterious police inspector arrives at the home of a wealthy industrialist. In the interrogation that follows, he eventually proves that all of the members of the family shared responsibility in the suicide of a desperate young woman who had been carrying the baby of one of the sons in the family. The two youngest children are stunned by their guilt, but their parents and the other family members convince themselves that the incident was merely a hoax. Although it is true that they have been callous and uncharitable to a particular young working-class woman, once they learn that the inspector was not really sent to see them by the local police, they are content to return to their superficial, hypocritical lives. As the play ends, they receive a call telling them that the young woman in question has in fact just died and that a real inspector is on his way to interrogate them. Priestley's message is that we are all members of a community and that we depend upon one another; if human beings cannot learn this lesson, then God will continue to teach it through fire, blood, and anguish.

Priestley's supernatural inspector has possibly been the direct source for similar characters in certain Spanish plays.[6] Such is not the case with Salom, although he does introduce a police inspector in several dramas, all of them related to Priestley in their moralistic tone and the emphasis placed on questions of individual responsibility and remorse. An Inspector Ruiz appears in *The Message, The Guilty, Lack of Evidence,* and *The Night of the Hundred Birds.* In spite of the repetition of name, the character is not always the same one. He is a realistic figure who functions sometimes as a police investigator, sometimes as a friend, and, to varying degrees, serves as a sounding board when the main character begins to appreciate the extent of his or her guilt. All four of these dramas deal with unhappy marriages which end in the death of one of the marriage partners. As the playwright has frequently noted, only one of them, *The Guilty,* falls completely within the format of a mystery play.

I   El mensaje

Salom's first play to be staged, *El mensaje* [The Message], was partially based on historical circumstance. In 1954, when the play was written, Spanish volunteers who had fought on the Russian front during World War II were released from Soviet concentration camps and returned home. The action revolves around a woman who, during her husband's long absence, has replaced him with someone else. The situation is, of course, not a new one in world literature and need not be identified with a particular moment in time. In Salom's version of the age-old story, Flora never really loved her husband Carlos, who had been her employer before she married him. Although she knows that he was taken prisoner and is alive, she and Augusto, a concert pianist, let everyone believe that Carlos is dead and that they are married.

As the play begins, Flora, unaware of the prisoners' release, has become alarmed that a man she believes to be Carlos's old enemy is following her in the streets. She calls her friend Inspector Ruiz to ask for his help. Ruiz laughs at her supposedly imaginary fears, but upon his departure, Germán enters from the balcony. He explains that he reformed his character, became Carlos's friend in prison, and brings her a message from her husband. It is clear to Flora that Carlos still loves her and she begins to feel remorse that his love has been unrequited. From this point forward, the action of the drama is built on a series of reversals. Ruiz returns to warn Flora that Germán is indeed in Spain and that he is wanted by the police; Flora now lies to protect Germán. In her guilt over Carlos, she rejects Augusto's love and he decides to go on a concert tour without her. Ruiz returns again and, with information he has learned from returning prisoners, proves to Flora that Germán is a liar and that Carlos is dead. In fact, Germán had escaped from prison a year before in Carlos's place, thus causing Carlos's punishment and death. Flora changes her mind and plans to rejoin Augusto, but Germán enters once again and convinces her that Carlos was a noble person who had actually sacrificed his life for Germán, his enemy. Transformed by remorse, Germán intends to turn himself in to the police. Flora elects to live alone with the memory of Carlos, her real husband. She realizes that she is responsible for his death; had she loved him, he would not have volunteered to fight the Russians and he would not have chosen to die in prison. As the play ends, Augusto calls her to find out why she is not at the train station, but she merely lets the phone ring.

The Message is marked by the structural characteristics of the "well-made play." Paced by the many entrances, exits, and telephone calls, the action moves briskly forward. The careful structure is somewhat contrived, particularly with respect to Germán's entrances from the balcony. Also somewhat contrived is the series of mysteries on which the action is based. In each of the three acts, with variations, the question is posed as to who Germán is and why he has come. Only in the third act do we find out what his real motivation is and only then does Flora find her true self. Both she and Germán have been deeply affected by the self-sacrifice and noble spirit of Carlos, a character who never appears on stage but whose actions nevertheless determine the outcome of the drama.[7]

Unlike Priestley's police inspector, Ruiz does not function as Flora's conscience. In fact, he offers her practical advice about forgetting the past. Flora, however, finds that she can no longer set aside her Catholic upbringing. When she is confronted both by Carlos's death and by his deep and abiding love for her throughout their years of separation, she realizes the full extent of her guilt and remorse. That her adultery took the form of a continuing relationship, a real marriage in the eyes of Flora and Augusto, only makes the sin now seem more monstrous to her. Her ultimate decision to remain faithful to the memory of Carlos and reject her lover when she is finally free to marry him in fact, is identical to the ending of the earlier *Mama's Smiling* and very consistent with the antidivorce stance that Salom was to take a few years later in *The Fourth Player*.[8]

II Culpables

Culpables [The Guilty], Salom's only murder mystery, was his first important theatrical success. Following its opening in Madrid in 1961, it was translated to several languages and staged in Germany, Belgium, Switzerland, Austria, and Czechoslovakia, as well as Latin America. It bears a clear thematic relationship to *The Message* in its treatment of adultery, guilt, and remorse, but its plot development is even more dependent upon sudden twists and surprises. Although the cast includes only five characters, the story is further complicated by the existence of two others who never appear on stage.

Andrés, a small-town doctor, is the lover of Silvia, wife of the wealthy businessman Rogelio. Although Silvia and Andrés normally meet in an apartment behind a fabric shop, she pretends to be a patient in order to see him at his office. Rogelio surprises them there and indicates that he has known about the affair all along but will help the lovers by "dying" provided that Andrés will sign a false death certificate. Having suffered financial reverses, Rogelio wishes to collect a large insurance policy by faking his death. The funeral takes place without difficulties but a year later, on the eve of the marriage of

Andrés and Silvia, police commissioner Ruiz appears to inform Andrés that his office in Madrid has received anonymous letters asserting that Rogelio was poisoned. At the insistence of the insurance company, the body will be exhumed. Much to Andrés's surprise, there is a body in the coffin; medical records prove the cadaver to be Rogelio. Afraid that Silvia has indeed killed her husband, Andrés confesses to Ruiz and asks him to find out the truth. The owner of the fabric shop is murdered, and it is assumed that Salvador García, Rogelio's partner in whose name the insurance money was sent outside Spain, is the culprit. Rogelio, however, reappears and confesses to Andrés that he is the murderer; in fact, he had killed García for telling him of Silvia's infidelity. Silvia had then invented the whole complicated plan, including burying García's body in Rogelio's grave and switching their medical records. Rogelio has written the anonymous letters and has returned because he loves his wife and wants her to go away with him. When Rogelio threatens to shoot Andrés, Silvia kills her husband.

Underlying the surface detective drama is Salom's habitual preoccupation with the moral implications of love and marriage. Silvia is a devious woman who has deceived her husband, lied to her lover, and masterminded an intricate scheme to conceal a murder and defraud an insurance company. Eventually she realizes that she is to blame for all of Rogelio's crimes. It was Rogelio's love for her and her adultery that caused the initial crime and that ultimately trapped them all. At the end she asks which of them was really the most guilty, clearly casting the responsibility on herself and Andrés, not on Rogelio. Andrés, while not implicated in the murders, has agreed to the fraud and has been guilty of adultery. As a doctor, he is particularly torn by guilt at signing a false death certificate. Ruiz's arrival not only frightens him but also causes him to begin questioning both his own moral responsibility and that of Silvia. Ruiz thus functions, on one level, like Priestley's inspector, as the catalyst to an awakened conscience.

On another level, Ruiz is a Sherlock Holmes–type detective who can arrive at quick and correct deductions based on relatively minor clues. For example, he knows that Silvia is a widow when he first meets her because of her wedding ring and he knows that García, a cigarette smoker, is not the murderer because of the smell of cigar smoke in the fabric shop and later in Andrés's office. The success of the drama is undoubtedly related to Salom's introduction of the clever detective, his adroit manipulation of the tangled threads of the plot, and his maintenance of an almost constant level of high suspense. The psychological analysis of his characters is less developed here than in the other plays of this group, making the moralistic conclusion seem somewhat gratuitous. *The Guilty* remains an entertaining detective story with no great literary value.

III   Falta de pruebas

Much more innovative in staging techniques and in the treatment of time is *Falta de pruebas* [Lack of Evidence], a drama that met with relative failure when it opened in Barcelona in 1964. *The Message* has a single stage setting; six of *The Guilty's* seven scenes take place in the same room. In both cases time is linear. These are very traditional plays in their construction, reflecting careful craftsmanship but little experimentation. *Lack of Evidence*, on the other hand, while strongly related to the two earlier works thematically, differs greatly from them in structure. In his comedy *The Great Adventure* (1961) Salom employed a simultaneous stage setting. In *Lack of Evidence* he extends this technique, utilizing a multiple stage setting to reveal simultaneously the interior of Adrián's modest apartment, a café, and a movie theater in a working-class neighborhood, the living room of Rogelio's elegant home, and the bar at a modern tennis club. The multiple stage setting became widely used in Spanish theater in the 1960s; Salom's setting here might be compared for example to that of Antonio Buero Vallejo's *El tragaluz* [The Basement Window, 1967]. Salom's experimentation with time, probably influenced by Priestley, is already present in his unpublished plays *Sleepless Night* and *The Fourth Player*.[9] In *Lack of Evidence* he introduces circular time, simultaneous action, and an extended flashback.

The basic story of *Lack of Evidence* and its revised version *The Night of the Hundred Birds* is essentially the same. Adrián as a young law student had courted Juana, a butcher's daughter. When her parents were suddenly killed in an accident, he married her in spite of their difference in social class, dropped out of law school, and worked with her in the meat stall at the market. His unhappiness and frustration are contained until he is invited to the twentieth reunion of his class; there he meets Lilián, a younger and far more elegant woman than Juana. He falls in love with her, not realizing that she is his classmate Rogelio's mistress. He plots to murder Juana by giving her an overdose of her heart medicine so that he may be free to marry

Lilián. Juana dies, but Adrián remains uncertain as to the real cause of her death. Did she take the medicine or did she die of a heart attack? If she took it, did she do so intentionally, sacrificing herself to his happiness? Regardless of his legal guilt, which cannot be proved, he finds himself morally guilty of a crime. Too late he realizes Juana's real worth and is overcome by remorse.

The question of moral guilt raised in the drama bears an obvious relationship to certain plays of Priestley as well as to other Spanish works that may similarly reflect the British playwright's influence. In *Dangerous Corner* Martin's death is accidental, but several of the characters share a moral responsibility in creating the situation that led to the fatality. The young woman in *An Inspector Calls* kills herself, but all of the members of the Birling family are indirectly guilty of her suicide. Retrospectively, the characters in both dramas are forced to probe the past and identify their roles in the deaths. José López Rubio's *Las manos son inocentes* [Our Hands Are Innocent, 1958] presents a situation almost identical to that of Salom's play. A couple attempt to poison their roomer and steal his money. He dies, but for a time it appears that he voluntarily poisoned himself so that they may inherit his estate. Ultimately it is learned that he died of natural causes. Like Adrián, the couple find themselves spiritually guilty; their intention to commit murder cannot be erased by the coincidence of a heart attack. As is also true with Adrián, their sense of remorse is only compounded upon realizing that their victim would have given his life to help them resolve their difficulties. Confronted by his burden of guilt, Adrián feels compelled to confess his crime. His confession is directed to the audience; this narration is in the present and serves to introduce the retrospective scenes from the past that enact the events leading up to Juana's death. The structure is somewhat different from that of Priestley's *An Inspector Calls*, where there is only one temporal plane, but is closely related to Víctor Ruiz Iriarte's *El carrusell* [The Carousel, 1964], which also alternates a confession in the present with the retrospective action from the past. In the case of Ruiz Iriarte's play, Daniel confesses his responsibility in a suicide not directly to the audience but rather to a commissioner who functions as conscience.[10]

Quite clearly *Lack of Evidence* falls within a current of serious drama that was popular in Spain in the 1950s and 1960s. The failure of Salom's play may be attributed not to its theme or its theatrical innovations but rather to its proliferation of characters, complications, and scenes. Its basic weakness is the one evident in several of the Catalan's earlier efforts such as *The Gray Hour* and *The White Triangle* where the overall impact of the play is similarly weakened by too many complications and subplots. The dramatic effect of *Lack of Evidence* is also diminished by the excessive use of Adrián's narration for the direct presentation of exposition and motivation.

The action of *Lack of Evidence* begins in the present with Adrián addressing his confession to the audience. Simultaneously, Juana and her friends pose for a picture that Adrián had taken at their anniversary a year before. The action switches to that moment of the past. The two temporal planes are then maintained as Adrián periodically returns to his direct narration in the present while episodes from the past are reenacted in dominantly chronological order. The alternation between the two moments in time is only broken significantly at the end of the play, when the action in the past reverts to its point of departure, namely, the anniversary party and the group photo.

While the fluidity of time is limited and carefully controlled, the movement in space is not. Scenes shift from Juana and Adrián's home to the café, to Adrián's chance encounter with Rogelio in the street, to the class reunion, etc. The marital difficulties of Rogelio and Carolina as well as his relationship with Lilián are made apparent in a scene involving the three of them. Episodes abound as extensive moments from the past are relived. For example, when Adrián takes Lilián's picture, the author presents a long segment related to their day together in the country. When Lilián proves to herself that Adrián is married by surprising him with Juana and their friends at a neighborhood movie, the scene, including part of the dialogue of the movie itself, is fully staged. The movie scene serves as the catalyst for Adrián's decision to murder his wife. The suggestion comes directly from the dialogue of the film while the physical juxtaposition of the elegant Lilián with the lower-class Juana convinces Adrián that his marriage and the vulgarity of his existence are intolerable. The act ends with Adrián's starting to give Juana an overdose of her medicine and then changing his mind because the crime would be too obvious.

In the second act, the action on the retrospective plane begins the night Juana dies. Adrián has been feigning a solicitous, affectionate attitude toward his wife in order to allay possible suspicions by their friends, particularly old Gustavo who has worked for Juana and her parents all of her life and Ruiz, a police inspector who had courted Juana before she married Adrián. Adrián leaves the overdose in the glass alongside Juana's bed while he goes off to the café; the action in the two locations is simultaneous. His careful plan is complicated first by his sudden remorse when Juana dies and then by the involvement of the maid Encarna, who has found Lilián's photo. Months later, when the wedding plans of Adrián and Lilián are announced in the newspaper, Encarna, jealous because Adrián has rejected her own amorous overtures, gives the photo to Ruiz and accuses Adrián of murder. Adrián, who in the meantime has met Carolina and learned from her that Lilián is Rogelio's mistress, willingly confesses to Ruiz. Whether or not he is legally guilty is now impossible to ascertain. An autopsy could no longer prove the actual amount of the medicine in Juana's body.[11] Moreover, Gustavo swears that the glass still had medicine in it when he emptied it in the sink after Juana's death. In truth, Gustavo does not know if Juana took the medicine or not; he falsifies his testimony to protect the man Juana loved because he knows that is what she would have wanted. Adrián is left with his moral guilt, his remorse, and his memories.

IV   La noche de los cien pájaros

By 1972 when the revised version of *Lack of Evidence* was staged in Madrid, Salom had greatly improved his skill as a theatrical craftsman. All of the extraneous elements in the earlier play are eliminated. The stage setting is simplified and the central action is more unified and cohesive. The number of characters is reduced from twelve to eight. The artificial exposition of Adrián's narration in *Lack of Evidence* is replaced by a more natural revelation of background and characterization within dialogue. A greater fluidity of time allows for a more effective use of irony and for a more vivid juxtaposition of Juana and Lilián and the worlds they represent to the anguished Adrián. The number of retrospective episodes is significantly decreased as Salom learns to evoke the essence of those scenes with a passing reference in the present or the briefest of flashbacks.

The most significant change between the two plays in plot development is the elimination from the cast of characters of both Rogelio and Carolina. The attention paid to Carolina and her psychological problems caused by Rogelio's infidelity detract from the treatment of the principal love triangle in *Lack of Evidence*.[12] In that Adrián is not initially aware of the Lilián–Rogelio–Carolina situation, the retrospective scenes involving them also break the intended structure of the drama which is built on Adrián's evocation of the past. In *La noche de los cien pájaros* [The Night of the Hundred Birds] Rogelio is merely mentioned as Adrián's former classmate and as one of Lilián's lovers; because he never appears, Adrián's courtship of Lilián no longer has the dimension of being a trap that Rogelio has deliberately laid for Adrián. Because Lilián is not seen feigning indifference for Rogelio in front of either Carolina or Adrián or both, her role is no longer limited to that of a stereotypical hypocrite. In fact, she becomes a much more interesting and complicated character in the later play. In addition to placing more emphasis on analysis of the major characters and less on the elaboration of detailed episodes, Salom has eliminated from *The Night of the Hundred Birds* certain other defects in the plot development of *Lack of Evidence*. Most notable among these is the deletion of the movie scene containing the melodramatic confrontation between Adrián's everyday reality and Lilián; also eliminated is the trite introduction through the film script of the suggestion that Adrián killed his wife.

Unlike *Lack of Evidence*, there is a single stage setting for *The Night of the Hundred Birds*. The scene is the apartment of Adrián and Juana. To provide spatial flexibility, some segments are acted on the apron without benefit of scenery; the minimal necessary changes of location—the nightclub for the class reunion in the first act and the café for the night of Juana's death in the second—are achieved by revolving the backdrop that forms the dining room wall. To a large extent audience imagination, special lighting, and music, as well as the actors' art, combine to replace the complex multiple stage setting of the earlier play. The action begins as the group picture is being taken at the anniversary party. The dialogue of this initial scene establishes Adrián's history as well as his dissatisfaction with his marriage and environment. Only at the end of the scene does it become apparent that the party and the photograph are from the past. On the temporal plane of the present, Adrián has brought Lilián to the apartment and is showing her the picture.

Salom's treatment of time in *The Night of the Hundred Birds* is both more fluid and more sophisticated than in the original version of the drama. Adrián's dialogue with Lilián in the present is a more dramatic and less contrived way of revealing his viewpoint than the narration in *Lack of Evidence*. Moreover, Lilián's visit to the apartment allows for concurrent action on the two temporal planes and hence a constant contrast between the two women. Within the retrospective scenes, which are consistently presented as the evocation of Adrián's memories, the action flows from one moment of the past to another. For example, when Juana reminds Adrián of a dance contest they had won years before, the sound of music and applause evokes that moment from a more distant past. It also serves as the transition forward in time to the dance floor at the class reunion where Adrián first met Lilián. Adrián has brought Lilián to his old apartment in response to Rogelio's revealing to him the truth about her love affairs. His intention is to force her to see his past and hence exchange truth for truth. Because his disillusionment with Lilián is apparent from the early minutes of the play, both the character and the audience are fully aware of the irony implicit in his rejection of the faithful and loving Juana for the other woman.

Salom's intention in *Lack of Evidence,* beyond developing his theme of moral responsibility, was to contrast the two social worlds represented by Juan and Lilián. He states in his self-criticism of the play that there is a constant juxtaposition of the lower middle class, which may be coarse and common but is also sincere and clean, with the shining outward appearance of the upper class: "Perhaps my work is only a modest voice of protest against the blind worship of external beauty and refinement to which our contemporary society seems to have surrendered, forgetting the true scale of human and moral values."[13] This aspect of the drama is given even greater emphasis in *The Night of the Hundred Birds* than in the original play. Juana's taste in clothes and in interior decorating are pointed out by Adrián for Lilián's negative reaction. Lilián is invited to ridicule Juana's fondness for appliances, her bourgeois commitment to the consumer society. Adrián converts Juana's dishwasher into a symbol of her and her social class. Unlike other Spanish plays of the early 1970s that attack the consumer society, works like Gala's *The Good Days Lost* (1972) or Ana Diosdado's *Usted también podrá disfrutar de Ella* [You, Too, Can Enjoy "Her", 1973], Salom tends to defend Juana's attitude. "Why can you feel proud of an abstract painting and not of the latest model machine?" Adrián asks Lilián.[14] Adrián, frustrated by his lot in life, offended by his wife's vulgarity, had longed for the hundred birds flying around him. He had sacrificed Juana, the bird in the hand, to that dream and now realizes the extent of his loss.

Juana is the best delineated of the three principal characters. She has, according to Adolfo Prego, more "vital eloquence."[15] She is an uncultured and coarse woman, but she is also a sensitive person and a

shrewd judge of character. She knows that Adrián is not content in
their marriage even as she reaches out to him for warmth and affection. For twenty years she has accepted the fact that he does not love
her the way she loves him, unselfishly and completely. The period of
time in which he prepares their friends for her death by showering
her with attention is the happiest for her of their life together. To
accept once again his indifference or scorn would be impossible. It is
at this point in their relationship that she proclaims, "Please never
stop loving me, Adrián, or look for another woman . . . if I didn't have
your love I think I would die" (N, 61). Does she deliberately take the
overdose of medicine when she realizes that Adrián wants her dead?
Probably, but Salom, in a Pirandellian touch, does not resolve the
ambiguity. In a sense, as Ruiz later tells Adrián, it does not matter;
one way or another, Adrián has caused Juana's death. "What do you
want me to tell you, that your deceit and your ingratitude were in
reality the true culprits?" (N, 70). The implication is that Juana's ill
health over the years had been aggravated by Adrián's attitude toward her. Significantly, during the second honeymoon—the period
preceding her death—her condition had improved. Salom, the
physician, is pointing out that a death by natural causes—i.e., a heart
attack—could well have been precipitated by the shock of realizing
that her husband was trying to kill her.

Adrián, too, is a well-developed character. Because we see him
simultaneously on two temporal planes—with Lilián in the present
and with Juana in the past—his sense of guilt and remorse are
constantly juxtaposed with his crime. When he learns that Lilián has
been the lover of Rogelio and other men, he responds in anger: "And
all for a whore like you! It was you I should have exterminated, not
her" (N, 41). At the end of the first act, he forces Lilián to undress; his
intention is to humiliate her by paying her for going to bed with him.
But Lilián is undoubtedly correct when she tells him that he did not
plan to kill Juana for her, "All that you did was in self-defense, in order
to recapture yourself" (N, 44). In fact, Adrián waited many weeks
after Juana's death before seeking out Lilián and proposing to her.
She had become a symbol for him of the life he might have had. The
class reunion and the meeting with an attractive and elegant younger
woman are merely the catalyst for his open rebellion against twenty
years of a stifling existence. He is, as Prego has observed, a man who
feels himself to be a failure and who yearns for some elusive happiness.[16] Learning the truth about Lilián's past has compounded the
remorse he already feels about Juana's death for now he knows that

the shining world he had reached out for is less genuine than the existence he willingly sacrificed. As the play ends, Adrián is immersed in his past. The characters are once again assembled for the anniversary picture. Lilián stands outside, knocking, but Adrián neither hears nor answers.

In *Lack of Evidence*, Lilián was a mere stereotype. In *The Night of the Hundred Birds*, she emerges as a third main character. On the surface she represents all of the bad aspects of a frivolous upper class that has forsaken traditional moral and spiritual values. She does look down upon Juana's life with scorn. Salom, however, portrays in her a more complex person. She is also a woman -who has never really known love and who longs to set aside her past just as Adrián wishes to forsake his. Rogelio realizes that she has fallen in love with Adrián in spite of, or more likely because of, his lack of sophistication. When she calls Rogelio to tell him that Adrián has proposed, she asks him not to laugh, then covers her face with her hands (*N*, 49). She would like Adrián to forget the truths they have learned about each other and look to a future together.

The Night of the Hundred Birds retains many of the same elements found in the earlier plays of guilt and remorse, including some characteristics of the detective story. It is, however, by far the most important drama in the group not only for its skillful use of theatrical techniques and its careful craftsmanship but even more so for its penetrating revelation of character. Fernando Lázaro Carreter has noted that it is within the "vein that Jaime Salom's talent handles best: that of the meticulous and loving psychological analysis of souls."[17] It is also the play that most effectively presents the moral that underlies *The Message* and *The Guilty* as well as the two versions of *Lack of Evidence*. When one betrays the person who loves him, eventually he must confront a guilty conscience. As Gustavo tells Adrián, "You don't need me to tell you the line between good and evil; you'll find it yourself" (*N*, 71).

CHAPTER 4

Three Early Comedies

IN THE beginning of his theatrical career, when he was still search-ing for the forms and themes that would provide the most appro-priate vehicles for his dramatic art, Salom turned frequently to comedy. The influences on these early efforts ranged from the parodies of detective stories then in vogue to the traditional *sainete* to a more profound kind of comedy, reflecting serious human concerns. In the period from December, 1960, to January, 1964, five of Salom's minor comedies, varying widely in tone and purpose, were staged in Spain.[1] Of this group, two, *The White Triangle* and *The Man with the Violin,* have remained unpublished. The remaining three, *Emerald Green, The Great Adventure,* and *Winter Games,* superior to the others in quality, are still relatively unimportant works in Salom's total theater. *Emerald Green* is a well-constructed, fast-moving mys-tery farce. *The Great Adventure* is Salom's only work written in Catalan; it is closely related to the *sainete* and has an obvious mess-age. *Winter Games* maintains many of the structural characteristics of light comedy or farce but treats the theme of death with sensitivity and, like *The Great Adventure,* presents a moral lesson.

I Verde esmeralda

In the years immediately after the Spanish Civil War, Enrique Jardiel Poncela (1901–1952) began writing comic detective plays. Typical of these was *Los ladrones somos gente honrada* [We Thieves Are Honest People, 1941]. Following his example and inspired by the mysteries of Agatha Christie, other Spanish playwrights soon fol-lowed suit; the trend continued throughout the 1950s and into the next decade. The most notable exponents of the popular comedies were Miguel Mihura, with such plays as *Carlota* (1957) and *Meloco-tón en almíbar* [Peaches and Syrup, 1958], and Alfonso Paso, who wrote many detective comedies including *Usted puede ser un asesino*

[You Can Be a Murderer, 1958] and *Receta para un crimen* [Recipe for a Crime, 1959].[2] These parodies of detective stories tend to use certain repeated comic techniques. They are marked by complicated plots filled with sudden twists and surprise solutions. If they are murder mysteries, the stage will become littered with corpses, whose presence evokes laughter rather than horror. Exploiting the comic effect resultant from incongruity, the playwrights will have their characters accept the terrifying or the outlandish as perfectly normal events. Often the characters are portrayed in role reversals: the clever detective will be easily outwitted, the professional thief will be the victim of robbery, the supposedly dumb character will ultimately solve the crime.

Salom's *Verde esmeralda* [Emerald Green], his first play to be staged in Madrid, is an entertaining farce that falls easily within the category of detective comedies. The cast is limited to five characters: Adolfo, a thief, and his wife Mariana; Fernando, a former private detective, and his older, wealthy wife Claudia; and Donata, the maid. The action takes place in the living room of Adolfo and Mariana. They have chosen this apartment so that they may be neighbors of Claudia and invite the couple over to facilitate stealing her emerald necklace from her safe. Adolfo's efforts are initially encouraged by Claudia's tendency to fall asleep when she is out visiting and by Fernando's obvious attraction to Mariana. Adolfo's first attempt is thwarted by the fact that Claudia is wearing the necklace under her cape. His second attempt yields even more surprising results; he comes home with the right jewel case, but instead of Claudia's necklace it contains one of Mariana's—stolen for her by Adolfo at an earlier date. Adolfo had accused the maid of being a thief when certain objects had disappeared, but it is now clear that the detective knows who he is and has turned the tables on him. In fact, Fernando plans to use the stolen goods in his possession as evidence of Adolfo's identity in order to have him arrested. Claudia, fearing that she will lose Fernando to Mariana if the younger woman's husband is in prison, returns the evidence to Mariana on the condition that she and Adolfo leave the country. Only at the end of the play do Mariana and Adolfo learn that the maid was Fernando's accomplice; they decide to take her with them anyway because good maids are hard to find.

The play is a fast-moving one filled with comic devices, situations, and dialogue. Adolfo is frequently forced to hide in closets and behind sofas, first to keep the maid from learning that he is the famous masked thief, the *Magpie*, and then, after he has insulted her and she threatens to quit, to keep her from finding out that he is not off on an extended trip. He sometimes appears in disguise, another stock comic device. Salom also exploits to the fullest the possibility for comic dialogue. For example, Adolfo expresses the price of things Mariana wants not in money but in time: a necklace like that could cost him twenty years. He is horrified when he thinks there is a thief in their house; "You can't trust anyone. . . . What is the world coming to!"[3] An ironic statement indeed, coming from Adolfo.

The primary basis of humor in the play stems, however, from role playing and role reversals. Adolfo is a famous jewel thief, but he is manipulated by his wife and forced to hide in closets to keep the maid from quitting. Fernando is a clever detective, but Mariana controls his amorous advances by making him do the Charleston by the hour—alone. All of the characters in the play have assumed roles; their realities are quite different from their superficial appearances. Mariana pretends an interest in Fernando so that Adolfo may steal the necklace. Fernando in turn pretends not to know this while he arranges to steal from Adolfo. The outraged maid is in fact a thief. But by far the cleverest character in the cast is Claudia, the woman who habitually dozes off and appears stupid but ultimately outwits them all, thief or detective. The real emerald necklace is in a bank vault in Switzerland; it has never been at risk, nor did she need to marry a detective to protect it. The emeralds they have so zealously guarded or sought are mere imitations. In the one moment in the play that transcends the comic tone, Claudia confesses to Mariana that she had wasted her youth by marrying an older but wealthy man; when he had died, she had repeated his mistake of trying to buy love. Mariana is sympathetic to Claudia and willingly helps her arrange the happy ending.

Emerald Green is a clever and entertaining mystery farce. Unlike some of Salom's other early plays, it has no superfluous scenes or characters but rather maintains the rapid pace that the subgenre demands. It evinces careful craftsmanship but little originality.

II La gran aventura

Poetic and sentimental, *La gran ventura* [The Great Adventure] is a *sainete* dealing with a lower-class family in a provincial city. It has been identified as falling within the Catalan tradition of popular comedies of manners, represented by playwrights such as Angel

Guimerá (1849–1924), Santiago Rusiñol (1861–1931), and Ignacio Iglesias (1871–1928).[4] Maurici, the main character, is a dreamer, a man who has always believed that he was born under a special star and will someday receive a letter telling him of a great adventure. He confides this dream at the beginning of the play to Mossèn Damià, the new and very young priest who has just arrived at the church where Maurici is sacristan. The sacristan's faith in fantasy and adventure is reflected in his daughter's name Alicia—inspired by *Alice in Wonderland*—and the names they choose together for two baby pigeons, Peter and Pan. His faith is also reflected in his daily ritual of waiting for Pasqual, the mail carrier, in hopes that the magic letter will finally come. While Maurici dreams, his wife Pilar and Alicia iron clothes from morning to night in order to earn enough money to keep bread on the table.

When the letter finally comes, it is the invitation to an obvious swindle. A woman Maurici knew briefly during the war and nicknamed Estrella—Star—writes him that she has inherited property in America; if he will provide a certain amount of money, they will go together to claim her fortune. Fidel, the café owner, warns Maurici that he is being tricked, but Maurici sells the land he inherited from his mother that was to be Alicia's dowry, steals candlesticks from the church, and forges Fidel's name to a check to raise the amount of money the woman demands. Even as he leaves for Barcelona to meet her, he knows that he is being victimized and in turn has betrayed his family, his friend, and his church. It is too late for him to change his mind, he tells Fidel; one thing leads to another and he finds himself hopelessly drugged by Estrella's love.

Only a few days pass before the disillusioned Maurici returns to his city and attempts to jump into the river. Mossèn Damià prevents the suicide before he realizes who the man is. Once he recognizes Maurici, he urges him to return to his family. A miracle awaits the prodigal son. His wife and daughter will cry tears of joy that he is back. Fidel will forgive him. A young priest will forget the candlesticks but will always remember the first soul he was able to save. The great adventure Maurici has yearned for is right in his own home.

The theme of illusion versus reality present in *The Great Adventure* is a common one in Hispanic literature. Specific parallels to Maurici's years of patient dreaming followed by deliberate deception may readily be found in Spanish theater. In López Rubio's *Alberto* (1949), for example, doña Elena lives with the illusion that her old sweetheart will eventually send for her; when he finally does, it is only because he wants her to take care of his motherless mulatto children. Similarly in Alejandro Casona's *La casa de los siete balcones* [The House with the Seven Balconies], staged in Buenos Aires in 1957, Tía Genoveva also waits for a letter to come from her sweetheart who has gone to America. When the letter finally arrives, it has been forged by her brother-in-law to trick her into leaving her home and giving him her fortune. The illusion of a great love or great adventure awaiting the character in all three comedies inevitably leads to disappointment.

The ending of Salom's play is idealized, as are the characters, to a large extent. Although the ambience is ostensibly that of poverty, the economic worries of Pilar seem to disappear as the play progresses. Alicia will marry the hard-working Pasqual. The squandered dowry will not matter. Maurici will not be prosecuted for his crimes. A comparison with a play like Lauro Olmo's *La camisa* [The Shirt], which also has some elements of the *sainete*, quickly reveals the relative lack of realism and social concern in Salom's comedy. *The Shirt* opened four months after *The Great Adventure* in Madrid and also deals with a poor family. In both plays the wife is far more practical than the husband, but in Olmo's work it is she who leaves home, not to chase an impossible dream but to seek employment as a maid in West Germany. In both plays, some characters hope for a miraculous change in their lives, but in *The Shirt* the harsh reality of their existences is made patently clear.

The Great Adventure and *The Shirt* are related in their use of stage settings. Marquerie has suggested that the multiple setting of *The Great Adventure* is, in fact, one of the best aspects of the comedy (102). More appropriately, it might be called a simultaneous setting. The backdrop and the stage itself are to represent various locations on a city square: the sacristy, the road, a café, a house, a bridge, a fountain, and a pigeon loft. In addition to these exterior locations, it is possible to move the house forward, remove the façade, and stage interior scenes. Although the setting, with its flexibility, might be considered innovative, simultaneous settings are not new; they were used in Elizabethan England, as well as in other European countries during the sixteenth and seventeenth centuries. Salom's modernized version of the simultaneous setting, like that of Olmo in *The Shirt*, allows him to create the atmosphere of a neighborhood while also developing the more intimate scenes within the home of his main characters. *The Great Adventure* is Salom's only play written in Catalan and his last work purely within the *sainete* tradition, but the experimentation with stage settings found here is developed further throughout much of his later theater.[5]

III   Juegos de invierno

Winner of the Isaac Fraga prize for 1963, *Juegos de invierno* [Winter Games] was undoubtedly the early comedy that added the most to Salom's growing reputation as a playwright. The principal characters are five men in an isolated old folks' home who are convinced that one of them will die before spring. Salom caricatures the men but nevertheless portrays them and their fears with tender humor. The oldest, the *Grandfather*, is clearly senile and is handled dominantly as a comic figure. The other four, however, are intended, as Marquerie has noted, to represent a microcosm of the human condition (123). The man nicknamed Lerroux holds leftist political views; he dreams of being called for important public office although in truth the position he once filled was a minor one and he is now too old. Even his ultraliberalism is not what he claims it to be; his entrance to the home was facilitated by a bishop's recommendation. His brother Juanín is a humble man, constantly insulted and browbeaten by Lerroux. Don Robertito claims to be a retired don Juan who squeezed life like a lemon, extracting as much as possible from it; the image he creates of his past is far different from the reality. Felix, in comic contrast with Lerroux, is the reactionary; he is also an embittered man who delights in shattering the illusions of others, thus serving as a foil to Robertito as well as to Lerroux.

Salom, in his self-criticism of the play, indicates that he has always felt a great fondness for old people: "They seem to me to be tender, touching, ingenuous. They are like children, but children without a future."[6] Indeed, the old men are treated like children by the other characters: doña Amparo, the director of the home; Lidia, the nurse; Martina, the maid; and the doctor. The diminutives Robertito and Juanín reinforce their childlike status. Unlike the old people in Ana Diosdado's more recent *El okapi* (1972), which similarly takes place in a nursing home, Salom's characters do not rebel. In their willingness to escape through illusion and to amuse themselves by quarreling, they are somewhat more closely related to the four old people in Ruiz Iriarte's *El landó de seis caballos* [The Six Horse Landau, 1950], although Salom's characters are generally more in touch with reality than Ruiz Iriarte's. They are all concerned with the possibility of imminent death. Thinking that having a doctor on the premises will afford them some protection against the winter, which has annually claimed a life at the home for the past twenty-four years, they advertise for one, planning to pay for his services themselves with some unexpected pension benefits. Their efforts are to no avail. On the very morning when spring is to arrive, when they believe that they have triumphed, Juanín quietly dies of a heart attack.

Repeatedly in his plays of guilt and remorse, Salom has shown individuals who failed to realize the true worth of their spouses until after their deaths. Similarly, Lerroux has always mistreated Juanín and taken him for granted while Juanín responded to his brother's insults with love. Even his reason for not wanting to die reveals his devotion: "I've never been good for anything, I know, but I'm your brother. . . . Who would take care of you? Who would bring you the chess set and polish your shoes each morning? Who would shave you? I've been shaving you for more than forty years. . . . Don't leave me, brother, don't!" (W, 19–20). Only when Juanín does not get up at his brother's command and it is apparent that he is dead does Lerroux recognize the extent of his loss: "Don't leave me alone, for God's sake, Juanín, don't die!" (W, 86).

The major flaw in *Winter Games*, as the critics noted at the time of its premiere, is that Salom does not limit himself to the poetic if sometimes farcical humor of his principal plot.[7] Interwoven is a subplot relating to the love relationship of the nurse, Lidia, and the doctor. In fact, he has answered the ad solely as a means of renewing an affair with her. His arrival at the home on a stormy night, the mysterious disappearance of his application, his nocturnal attempts to enter her room from the balcony, the secret plans of the old men to kill the doctor in order to protect Lidia's honor, have all the earmarks of the detective comedy. The subplot is further complicated by the attitude of doña Amparo, a frustrated old maid who resents Lidia's youth and warmth. When Juanín dies, doña Amparo tears up Lidia's letter of resignation and forgives her her past indiscretions. The character of Lidia herself is again reminiscent of Ruiz Iriarte's *The Six Horse Landau*. Like Isabel in the earlier comedy, Lidia is content to sacrifice her youth in order to bring happiness to the old people. Fortunately, in both cases, the men who love the young women are willing to join them in their altruistic ventures. Lidia's devotion to the old men and their love for her neither destroy the unity of the play nor detract from the development of the main plot. The critics are undoubtedly correct, however, in asserting that the melodramatic over-tones of Lidia's love affair and conflict with doña Amparo as well as the extent that this subplot imposes itself on the principal action do prevent *Winter Games* from being one of Salom's more significant achievements.

Winter Games cannot easily be grouped with other works of the Catalan playwright, but it does have some points in common with certain of the early plays. The implicit moral lesson concerning death and remorse is the same one expressed more openly in the Inspector Ruiz plays. The partial use of detective story elements may similarly be related to those dramas and to *Emerald Green*. Like *The Great Adventure*, *Winter Games* makes use of a simultaneous setting, this time one that represents the interior, the porch, and the garden of the old folks' home. More importantly, *Winter Games*, with its sym-pathetic and tender portrayal of the elderly, anticipates Salom's first major triumph, *The Trunk of Disguises*, whose protagonist is an old man given the miraculous opportunity of reliving parts of his life.

CHAPTER 5

Plays of Poetic Fantasy

IN 1964 *El baúl de los disfraces* [The Trunk of Disguises] achieved major success in both Barcelona and Madrid, at last establishing Salom as one of contemporary Spain's important playwrights. Innovative in structure and staging technique, it is a work of poetic fantasy that represents a new point of departure in the Catalan's theater. Through the use of doubling, the cast of three actors is able to portray a number of characters in a series of episodes evoking the main character's past. Similarly in *Parcheesi Party* (1965) and its revision *Saturday Night Date*, (1967), four actors play multiple roles in order to present one character's imaginary adventures. Because of their episodic structure, these three comedies may be classified as anthology plays, that is, collections of skits or self-contained scenes connected by some unifying thread. A fourth comedy of poetic fantasy, *Trip on a Trapeze* (1970), continues the use of doubling but presents the role-playing as an integral component of plot and character development.

Salom has called *The Trunk of Disguises* his first authentically original work, and can identify no specific influence for his use of actors in multiple roles. "As for the doubling of my characters, I have never really thought about it. It has no antecedents and was born by spontaneous generation, because I felt it intuitively. Perhaps my being a doctor has made me see the human being from different angles, influenced by external circumstances and situations."[1] Although Salom's particular use of doubling reflects his own creativity, the technique itself dates back to the origins of Greek tragedy when the playwright, through the use of masks, was able to assign all of the roles to himself. Later, when the second and third actors were introduced, they generally divided the secondary parts between them. Into the twentieth century, doubling has continued to be a common practice, most frequently in plays requiring a large cast in order to reduce the number of actors needed for minor roles. Salom uses doubling for neither economic nor logistical convenience; rather he introduces it not only in the works of poetic fantasy but in some of his later plays as well in order to achieve an artistic effect or underscore a philosophical or psychological concept. In all cases, the technique is a theatricalist one, reminding the audience that what they are seeing is not reality.[2]

I   El baúl de los disfraces

The background for *The Trunk of Disguises* is carnival and a masquerade party; accordingly, one critic has called the comedy a "midwinter's night dream."[3] Indeed, the basic premise of the plot is a fanciful one, evoking the magical quality associated with Shakespeare's *A Midsummer's Night Dream* or Spanish works dealing with St. John's Night. Juan has been relegated to the library by his grandson, who fears that the old man will get in the way during his party. But *Ella*, the grandson's date, visits Juan and convinces him that his old age is nothing but a disguise that he can remove at will. With her help and the costumes from a hidden trunk, Juan becomes once again a sentimental student, a young army officer, and a fifty-year-old man. In each of the episodes, *Ella* becomes the woman Juan loved at that point in his life. To Juan's dismay, at the end of the night only one costume remains in the trunk: the very one of old age that he wore at the beginning. It is, *Ella* says, the costume found "in the back of every closet and at the bottom of every trunk."[4] She understands that Juan feels sad and lonely, but his situation is a natural stage of life. When the grandson reaches Juan's age, he, too, "will remember me, alone in the library, as you have remembered me" (*T*, 147).

The roles played by *Ella* in the three retrospective episodes vary. When Juan is a young student, she is a Spanish café singer. When he is an army officer, she is Austrian, the wife of a visiting colonel. In the third episode, she is *Gatita*, Juan's young mistress. In spite of the changes in costume, characterization, and even nationality, *Ella* is always the same. The technique of doubling is clearly intended to reinforce the symbolic nature of the feminine figure. As she explains to Juan, "Illusion has no age, no nationality, no logic. I was always love, Juan. . . . That impossible love that comes and goes . . . " (*T*, 111).

While the actor portraying Juan must be able to create four life stages of the same character and the actress must be able to differentiate convincingly several guises of the eternal feminine, to the third actor—*El Otro*—falls the challenging task of creating five unrelated male characters. In keeping with the carnival background, as the grandson he appears in the costume of Pierrot. In the first episode, he is Dupont, the middle-aged French owner of the café where *Ella* sings; he is also her lover and obviously exploits the young woman. In the second episode, he is Juan's military commander, taking no direct part in the love story. The third episode is an inversion of the first. *El Otro* is now a medical student who pretends to be a doctor when he falls in love with *Gatita* in order to be allowed to enter her apartment. Juan, who as a student had tried unsuccessfully to win the café singer away from Dupont, is now the older man who thinks that he can thwart young love and buy affection. After *Gatita* languishes away and dies, *El Otro* once again appears, this time as an employee of a funeral home.

Underlying *The Trunk of Disguises* is a poetic if somewhat melancholy view of the human condition. *Ella* has been that "little light of illusion" (*T*, 148), coming from time to time over the years, for which Juan is grateful; but inevitably the illusion is lost, and the youthful heart succumbs to the aging body. As the grandson, *El Otro* is embarking upon the same cycle. In his self-criticism of the play, Salom has said that Life itself is the real protagonist, "that slow and implacable passage of time that makes us put on each day an older disguise than we wore the day before."[5] The surface action of the play, however, is comic, even farcical, thus avoiding excessive sentimentality. Several of the roles, particularly those played by *El Otro*, are clearly caricatures. The various theatricalist staging techniques similarly prevent the audience from becoming emotionally involved as they might in a more realistic work.

The setting is a library with a door leading to a garden. Scene changes are accomplished either by calling upon the audience's imagination or by turning revolving bookcases to reveal the trunk, the café stage, or a bedroom. Transitions from one moment in time to another are facilitated by original poems and songs that parody the popular works of the particular period. All but one of Juan's costume changes as well as some of *Ella's* are made on stage; the doubling is thus an overt technique, intended to emphasize the theatricalism of the play. *Ella* occasionally speaks directly to the audience; she and Juan maintain a commentary in the present, simultaneous with their retrospective scenes. Both of these devices also make it clear that the actors are deliberately playing roles.

In keeping with the nonrepresentational nature of *The Trunk of Disguises*, Salom places heavy demands on both actors and audience.

He evokes imaginary characters, settings, and scenes. Days or weeks of activity may be telescoped into a few lines of dialogue. He explains in his self-criticism that he attempted to eliminate everything he considered unnecessary or merely accessory. In the first retrospective episode, Juan goes to the café with his fiancée and her family; as these characters do not appear, Juan must create them for us. In the third episode, he similarly consults a series of doctors about *Gatita's* illness; only his half of the conversations is given. The most striking use of this kind of theatricalist device comes in the second episode, when Juan goes to the railroad station to meet the colonel's wife and take her to her hotel in a landau. The railroad station is created for the audience through special sound effects and Juan's speech. The landau is really a table; the actors rock back and forth to create the impression that they are moving.

Marquerie quite correctly notes (249) that the imaginary landau in *The Trunk of Disguises* is related to the truck in *Motor Running* and that the device has an antecedent in the theater of Thornton Wilder (1897–1975). In his one-act play *The Happy Journey to Trenton and Camden* (1931), the American playwright uses four chairs set on a low platform to serve as the automobile in which his family goes for a ride; there is no scenery.[6] On the Spanish stage, Ruiz Iriarte also introduced an imaginary carriage in his *The Six Horse Landau*; his characters, immersed in their own world of poetic fantasy, are able to pretend that a sofa is really a horse-drawn carriage. Unlike the Wilder and Salom plays, however, Ruiz Iriarte does not expect his audience to participate in the illusion with his characters.

Given the theatricalist nature of *The Trunk of Disguises,* this comedy (as well as Salom's other works of poetic fantasy) bears certain resemblances to Wilder and other proponents of a nonrepresentational theater, such as Luigi Pirandello (1867–1936) and Nikolai Evreinov (1879–1953).[7] The ties between *The Trunk of Disguises* and Wilder are particularly strong. The role of *Ella,* with her direct address to the audience and her guidance of Juan through the retrospective scenes, might be compared to the Stage Manager in *Our Town* (1938) and Emily Webb's return—after her death—to her twelfth birthday party. Both plays have an episodic structure, and both present with sadness the passage of time and people's inability to take full advantage of their lives. Salom's comedy, however, is not a mere adaptation of Wilder's techniques and philosophy. Salient characteristics of *The Trunk of Disguises*—the use of doubling, songs, and elements of farce—have no counterparts in *Our Town.*

Because poetic fantasy is an important current of twentieth-century theater, it is not surprising that *The Trunk of Disguises* may also be compared to other Spanish plays. Most closely related to it in structure and technique is Ruiz Iriarte's *Un paraguas bajo la lluvia* [An Umbrella Under the Rain, 1965], an anthology play that premiered in Madrid a year after Salom's comedy opened in the capital city. In Ruiz Iriarte's work, his main character, from the perspective of the present, is able to witness the love triangles in which her great-grandmother, her grandmother, and her mother were involved in various moments from the past. The same three actors portray the roles of Florita, her prey, and her rival in the retrospective scenes as well as in the resolution of the current Florita's problem. The use of doubling is quite similar to that in *The Trunk of Disguises*, including its implicit message that each generation will experience the same kind of love as the previous one. Florita is guided through the past by her mother's ghost, a figure thus related to *Ella* both in her structural role in the play and in her supernatural character. In both plays, the authors use music to aid in the transition from one period of time to another. Ruiz Iriarte, however, makes more extensive use of lighting effects in order to shift the action from one section of the stage—a platform on which Florita and the ghost converse in the present—to another—the scene of the various love stories. This last staging technique is one that Salom incorporates in his later *Saturday Night Date*.

Although *The Trunk of Disguises* excels in its use of modern theatrical devices, it also reflects long-standing traditions in farce. Marquerie has pointed out the relationships with the *commedia dell'arte*, Lope de Rueda, and Molière (250–53). The grandson appears in the stock costume and mask of Pierrot; *Ella* likewise assumes the traditional mask. She actually maintains two roles in the present, that of the grandson's date and that of the eternal feminine. To some extent, she differentiates between the two by changing from a red mask to a black one. Similarly, Salom makes use of stock comic situations. The alleged doctor in the *Gatita* episode pretends to diagnose her disease, falsifies a prescription, and tricks Juan into taking the medicine; it is a classic scene, repeated with variations in the *commedia dell'arte* and throughout the history of farce.

Salom's return to the characters and masks of the *commedia dell'arte* not only relates his comedy to nonrepresentational theater of other centuries but also to the theatricalist plays of Evreinov. The Russian's most important play, known as *The Main Thing* in English and translated to Spanish in 1928 by Azorín under the title *El doctor Frégoli o La comedia de la felicidad* [Doctor Fregoli or the Comedy of Happiness], ends with a carnival scene in which Fregoli appears in the guise of Harlequin. Fregoli in fact appears in several different roles during the various episodes of the play. Three other characters are actors who enact parts as Fregoli theatricalizes life in order to bring happiness to others. The essential difference between Evreinov's use of doubling and Salom's is that the former results in a play within a play, deliberately staged by Fregoli without the knowledge of some of the characters, while the latter is a theatrical technique not intended to create an illusion internal to the comedy itself.

The Trunk of Disguises was Salom's first major triumph and remains one of his most important works. In addition to its careful structure and integration of various innovative techniques, the comedy reveals a delicate balance between the serious and the comic, the sentimental and the farcical. Salom portrays the elderly Juan with compassion and tenderness, but he constantly blends the melancholy undertones with a surface laughter. *The Trunk of Disguises* is at once a complex theatrical game, a lighthearted farce, and a poetic commentary on the human condition.

II Parchís Party

Although *Parchís Party* [Parcheesi Party] is a continuation of the theatrical techniques introduced in *The Trunk of Disguises*, it is nonetheless a play that repeats the basic structural error of some of Salom's earlier efforts. Rather than limit himself to essential elements, evoking the various episodes in an impressionistic way as he did so successfully in *The Trunk of Disguises*, Salom attempts to develop subplots too fully, thus slowing the action of the play and detracting from the comic effect. As one critic noted at the time, "The protagonist tells her story with an excessive amount of details, the transitions between anecdotes are too long, the changes of costume are cumbersome, the adventures are either too lengthy and drawn out or fall into trivial jokes."[8] The comedy offered possibilities, but in this original version, Salom had not yet found the appropriate technique for presenting his character and her fantasies.

Leoncia, the main character of *Parcheesi Party*, is a provincial housewife. The one escape from her humdrum existence is the Saturday night parcheesi game which she and her husband Felipe play each week with their friends Agapito and Ramona; as the two couples play, Leoncia's mind wanders and she experiences a series of imaginary adventures in which she sees herself as a *femme fatale*. The basic premise of the comedy has been compared with James Thurber's *The Secret Life of Walter Mitty*.[9] During the course of the play, Leoncia imagines four adventures, each of them precipitated by some news story of the day mentioned in the couples' conversation or on the radio. The four actors double in the various roles required by the episodes. The adventures are loosely connected by Leoncia's imagination and her sense of sexual frustration. In each of the four skits she casts Agapito as her lover or the man she plans to seduce, while generally reducing Ramona, a woman she obviously resents, to a subservient position—either as Leoncia's maid or as the wife Agapito is willing to deceive. Similarly, Felipe is reduced to an inferior position in three of the plays-within-a-play—as an effeminate or deceived husband or as a beggar. The use of doubling is intended to reveal a psychological truth about the main character. But Salom fails to emphasize the constant identity of the main characters within the daydreams; the adventures thus lack the strong unifying thread of *The Trunk of Disguises*.

The four interpolated adventures are self-contained scenes satirizing several unrelated aspects of contemporary society. In the first, Leoncia is an American millionairess who has come to Spain to build a shirt factory; Agapito is so eager to be her factory director that he is willing to become Leoncia's lover or to allow Leoncia's husband Felipe to become his wife's lover in order to secure the high-salaried position. The second episode, which in its reversal of roles is somewhat reminiscent of Ruiz Iriarte's *Cuando ella es la otra* [When She Is the Other Woman, 1951], depicts Leoncia as a "virtuous" kept woman who sends her lover back to his liberated wife in order to help his daughter marry well.[10] In the third adventure, Leoncia is a Spanish nurse in a Scandinavian hospital; Agapito is a patient whose vocabulary is limited to the one word "brijobsol" but whose amorous interest in the nurse is readily apparent. Leoncia, who is desirous of getting married, would be happy to take her blond admirer back to Spain, but the Northern hospital bureaucracy unfortunately declares him dead. The tangled but farcical plot is intended to spoof dehumanized technology and probably socialism as well. The final fantasy has Leoncia in the role of an Italian movie actress who has left her middle-class dentist husband to become the lover of a film director. When her movies start to lose money, she and Agapito attempt to have her husband cause a scandal in order to give them the greater notoriety that will make her a box office attraction again.

Parcheesi Party does not display the same skillful use of staging techniques that Salom had shown in *The Trunk of Disguises*. The imaginary adventures are not so well blended into the basic story line; in fact Salom marks each of them with a poster, labeling the scenes "Money," "Virtue," "The System," and "Art." In other respects as well, the action does not flow easily from one plane of reality to the other. Leoncia's seat is a special one that can be raised when she embarks on an imaginary adventure. It may become the airplane in which she is arriving or departing, or it may simply indicate that she is off in the clouds. Apparently hesitant to rely fully on the audience's collaboration in spite of the essential theatricalism of the play, Salom has his characters exit between some of the scenes in order to make costume changes and introduces props and pieces of scenery in addition to the posters in order to show changes of locale. The resultant staging is sometimes awkward and unquestionably contributed to the comedy's initial lack of success.

III Cita los sábados

The revision of *Parcheesi Party, Cita los sábados* [Saturday Night Date], proved much more successful than the earlier comedy and put an end to the series of relative failures which followed the triumph of *The Trunk of Disguises*. The original production opened in March, 1967, and won the Barcelona Critics' prize. In 1968 Ismael Merlo and Vicky Lagos took the play on a tour of various provincial capitals; in the summer of 1969, Salom staged the comedy a second time in Barcelona at his own Moratín theater. A subsequent Madrid production in the fall of 1973 achieved a respectable run of more than one hundred performances.

In rewriting his poetic fantasy, Salom added musical numbers, substituted two new episodes, and simplified the staging techniques. Relying more extensively on the audience's imagination, he eliminated both the posters labeling the adventures and Leoncia's movable seat. The transition from one plane of reality to the other is achieved with greater fluidity. As Marquerie observed, "The light marks the steps and transitions from the real to the illusionary, only the light and the changes of dress, and not—we repeat—other recourses or scenic devices and materials that were used in *Parcheesi*

Party. It is a kind of act of scenic humility, a practical application of the theories and principles of Grotowski about 'Poor Theater'" (Marquerie, 268).[11]

In both versions of the comedy the frame for the various episodes is the marriage of Leoncia and Felipe. Caricaturing the rigid moral views of the traditional Spanish woman, Salom has Leoncia restrict the couple's lovemaking to Tuesday nights. At the end of the play, when Leoncia realizes both that her daydreams result from sexual frustration and that her attitude may push Felipe into adultery, the couple happily declares Saturday to be a Tuesday. The comedy is thus filled with a certain amount of slightly erotic humor that might be compared to that of French vaudeville or to Spanish plays like Ruiz Iriarte's *An Umbrella Under the Rain*. The mildly risqué humor is more fully exploited in *Saturday Night Date* than in *Parcheesi Party* and becomes the unifying thread for the various episodes. Reinforcing Leoncia's frustration is her resentment of Ramona, who prides herself on looking like Marilyn Monroe and whose husband constantly showers her with affection. A comic conflict between the two women is maintained throughout the scenes taking place on the level of reality. Leoncia responds to the other woman's physical attributes and overtly affectionate husband with her motherhood and her fame as a pastry cook. The Leoncia–Ramona conflict similarly underlies the imaginary sequences. In *Saturday Night Date*, Salom effectively gives greater emphasis to this aspect of Leoncia's fantasy and hence greater unity to the imaginary adventures than in *Parcheesi Party* by eliminating the scenes satirizing Scandinavian bureaucracy and foreign capital investment in Spain.

In *Saturday Night Date* Salom also exploits more fully the theatricalist techniques introduced in *Parcheesi Party*. Leoncia, like the Stage Manager in Wilder's *Our Town*, serves as a kind of narrator who directs herself to the audience. She not only clarifies her own thoughts in this way but also introduces episodes or functions as a director controlling the actions of the actors. For example, in shifting from the plane of reality to that of fantasy for the fourth episode, Leoncia has the other actors freeze in their positions. They come back to life in the dream sequence and then revert to immobility as she indicates the return to reality. The transition to three of the four episodes is handled on stage, with the minimal costume changes required being done in full view of the audience.[12] Additionally, the transitions are facilitated by the series of original songs set to music by

Luis Aguilé; the musical numbers clearly enhance the entertainment value of the comedy, giving it the same kind of music-hall flavor found in *The Trunk of Disguises.*

The first of Leoncia's four dreams is one that did not appear in *Parcheesi Party.* From the couples' conversation about a dance hall star whose picture appears in the newspaper, Leoncia decides that she looks like the famous Tatá Bombón. In Leoncia's fantasy, Ramona remains herself; she merely sits on the couch watching the two men assume a variety of roles as Tatá Bombón–Leoncia's admirers. The farcical sequence, which has no plot, moves at a rapid pace. The episode is carefully blended into the main play not only by having the characters discuss Tatá Bombón prior to the imaginary adventure but also by having Tatá Bombón–Leoncia praise the fame and virtues of Leoncia within the dream. At the end of the fantasy, Ramona "dies" on the couch while on the other plane of reality she has been "killed" in the parcheesi game.

The "virtuous kept woman" episode of *Parcheesi Party* is the only imaginary adventure to appear virtually unmodified in the revised comedy.[13] Salom does, however, improve the transition to this particular fantasy. Leoncia is so shocked by the immorality of her imaginary life-style in the Tatá Bombón sequence that she promises the audience to daydream about herself as a good and virtuous woman for a change. It is only at the end of the episode that Leoncia's old servant Ramona and the audience realize that Leoncia, not the "other woman" for whom Felipe abandons her, is the woman of easy virtue. The surprise ending thus has a greater comic effect than in the earlier comedy and also reinforces the theme of Leoncia's sexual frustration.

The second act begins with a modified version of the Italian movie star episode from *Parcheesi Party.* Taking advantage of a stock comic device, Salom has Leoncia and Agapito use words and phrases in Italian. He also revises the episode to have Ramona and Felipe clearly double as themselves transposed to Leoncia's world of fantasy. Ramona is still Leoncia's maid, but her name and identity are those of the provincial housewife. Felipe is also himself—the owner of a lingerie shop in a small town. In Leoncia's daydream she has thus left her husband to become a famous film actress and the lover of Agapito, now a film director. Ramona, in her similar search for adventure, is capable only of serving as Leoncia's maid. The source of the fantasy is a radio drama that the couples listen to during their parcheesi game. In another theatricalist device, Salom has the actors within the fantasy sequence step up to an imaginary microphone, thus doubling also as the radio voices.

The final interpolated episode is the most overtly bawdy of the four daydreams. Ramona and Leoncia are now prostitutes. Agapito is Ramona's pimp, and Felipe is a provincial visitor to the city who specifically seeks out the professional services of Leoncia. Agapito believes throughout the farce that he is taking advantage of Felipe's innocence and will soon separate him from the sizeable roll of money that he is carrying. The money, however, is Leoncia's inheritance and Felipe, not at all innocent, has tricked Leoncia and the other two into satisfying his desire for wine, women, and song for free.

Saturday Night Date, even more than *Parcheesi Party*, is intended to be light entertainment. The tone throughout is that of farce, and the characters, even on the plane of reality, tend to be caricatures. Leoncia and Ramona in particular are stereotypes, catty women who feign friendship but view each other as rivals for the two men's attentions. *Saturday Night Date* does represent an important step forward in Salom's theater, for it incorporates quite skillfully techniques that are repeated in his later plays. Noteworthy among these are the theatricalist staging with its fluidity of movement from one plane of reality to another and the use of doubling to visualize the psychological concerns of a character. Although the comedy does not present as obvious a commentary on the human condition as *The Trunk of Disguises*, it does underscore Salom's continuing concern for empty lives and unfulfilling marriages.

IV   Viaje en un trapecio

Called a "game in two acts" by the playwright, *Viaje en un trapecio* [Trip on a Trapeze] is in several ways the most complex and interesting of the four works of poetic fantasy. The underlying theme once again is love, but the sentimentality of *The Trunk of Disguises* and the lighthearted ending of *Saturday Night Date* have disappeared. Beneath the surface game of *Trip on a Trapeze* is a story tinged with bitterness and disillusionment. The anthology format of the earlier comedies has also yielded to a more sophisticated approach to doubling; the transitions from one plane of reality to another are marked by great fluidity as the characters self-consciously play a series of roles. Completely theatricalist in its staging techniques, *Trip on a Trapeze* is the most Pirandellian of the Catalan's plays.

The comedy opened in November, 1970, in the Moratín theater in Barcelona and is the only one of Salom's mature works that has never been staged in the capital. Like the author's other plays of poetic fantasy, it has a very small cast—two actors and one actress—and like *The Trunk of Disguises* and *Saturday Night Date,* it introduces several musical numbers featuring Salom's original lyrics. The female roles in *Trip on a Trapeze* were created by Amparo Soler Leal, the same actress who appeared in both the Barcelona and Madrid productions of *The Trunk of Disguises.*

The background for *Trip on a Trapeze* is a traveling circus.[14] The stage setting is reduced to a minimum: a circus wagon, a window, a bench, a small circus ring, a tree. The atmosphere of the circus is evoked impressionistically, primarily as a metaphor which allows Salom to present multiple planes of reality. Reminiscent of Pirandello, who often used the theater as the background for his dramas, Salom thus is able to develop a play-within-a-play in which the fine line between theater and life begins to blur.

The comedy opens with a prologue directed to the audience by Patapluf, the clown. He announces that, because the other performers have left the circus, César and Estrella will play all of the parts. Creditors have stripped the circus bare, but no one can take away César and Estrella's own story. The story is one of unrequited love. Estrella, an eighteen-year-old waitress in Schmitt's bar, fell in love with César, but César married the great circus star Laura. Laura in turn was the lover of Schmitt, an odious man who exploited her and loved no one but himself. César continues to love Laura even after she abandons him to go away with Schmitt and even after Estrella becomes his lover. César and Estrella in their reenactment portray both themselves in the past and their rivals. In parallel with their story is that of Patapluf and his dog Plim. Plim is as faithful to his master as Estrella is to César, but Patapluf beats the dog and showers his affection on a white rat, Bibí. Although he does not do so himself, Delgado correctly suggests that the relationships among the characters could be diagramed (lviii–lix):

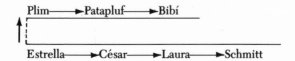

The obvious correlations between the two parallel stories are, as Delgado notes, Estrella–Plim, César–Patapluf, and Laura–Bibí. These are also the parallels directly expressed in the play. When Laura leaves César, Bibí disappears from his cage. Estrella clearly identifies with Plim, commenting to him, "You are nothing but a poor lonely creature who, like me, has finally found someone to love."[15] On one level of reality, Estrella and Plim both die when they must face the truth that their love will never be returned. Plim ate Bibí, but even without his rival present, he cannot gain Patapluf's affection. Estrella tried to kill César's love for his unfaithful wife by projecting her negative image of Laura onto César's consciousness, but when Laura returns, César leaves Estrella. Only when it is too late does César realize his error: "That cretin of a clown has just destroyed the only being in the world capable of loving him. And I . . . , well, I have been just as much of a cretin as he" (V, 479).

The interrelationships among the characters are more complex than this one series of parallels. Estrella loves Plim and attempts to protect the dog from his master's hostility, but Plim remains loyal to Patapluf. "We dogs love our masters, you know. It's our instinct. We cannot change," he tells her (V, 463). Plim's love for Patapluf is like that of Estrella for César, but it is also like that of César for Laura. Estrella tries to protect both Plim and César from the cruelty of Patapluf and Laura but she is not successful in reversing the direction of their loyalty and love. Throughout most of the comedy, Plim is a stuffed animal, but in one scene the dog comes to life with César doubling in the role. Similarly, there is a parallel not only between Laura and Bibí but also between Laura and Patapluf and, in turn, between Bibí and Schmitt. The latter two characters are incapable of loving anyone but themselves. Laura–Patapluf mistreat the faithful César–Plim but will receive no real warmth or affection from the objects of their own love.

In his self-criticism of the play, Salom asserts that the trapeze of the title represents the movement between planes of reality and fantasy. The characters attempt to go off into the clouds of illusion, but the implacable laws of physics bring them, like the trapeze, back to earth, preventing any authentic escape.[16] Indeed, the action of the play and the characterizations are noted for their oscillation. Not only do Estrella and César swing back and forth between their roles as themselves and their roles as Laura and Schmitt, but they also shift constantly between an idealized vision of themselves in the past and their "realities." Their love story is subject to the same kind of swinging action as is their role playing. At the time of the Barcelona premiere, one critic saw the trapeze motion to be symbolic of the "eternal zigzagging journey" of any amorous feeling or of the "dizzying instability in that narrow circle that is human life."[17]

The oscillation between illusion and reality begins with the first scene of the play. César appears as the circus ringmaster, explaining that the audience is about to witness the most fascinating, cruel, sweet, tragic, tender, grandiose spectacle on earth: Love (V, 409–10). He proceeds to identify himself as an egotistical and stupid man. Patapluf interrupts, objecting that César's self-characterization will displease Estrella and that it is an improvisation. It is readily apparent that the play-within-a-play, that is, the announced story of César's love, is a performance to be presented according to a planned script. As the performance continues, the characters interrupt repeatedly, as Patapluf does in this first scene, interjecting their individual interpretations of reality. When Estrella first appears as Laura, César informs the audience that she is not the real Laura. Estrella in turn interposes her opinion of Laura, a viewpoint quite different from the romanticized image César would like to present. Truth is relative; throughout much of the play Salom juxtaposes the differing perspectives of César and Estrella, thus creating a kind of Pirandellian ambiguity.

Although the audience is made aware from the prologue on that César and Estrella are deliberately playing roles and hence that part of what is staged is theater, not life, the full extent of the illusion is not clear until the final scenes. Patapluf's comment at the beginning creates the impression that Estrella loves César and for that reason will be angry if he says negative things about himself. When Estrella appears to die in the play-within-a-play, César rejects Laura and realizes that he has loved the wrong woman. The stage is set for a clarification that Estrella is alive after all and that she and César have found happiness. Estrella destroys this illusion by insisting upon revealing the authentic ending to their poor love story even though César says both that the truth will ruin the spectacle and that the audience does not care whether the ending is authentic or not. Estrella's truth is that upon Laura's return, César abandoned the younger woman, thus forcing her into prostitution. Years later she and César were reunited, but by then it was too late for them to find happiness: "You never loved me. And I stopped loving you a long time ago" (V, 484). Not only is their love story not what it seemed to be, but Patapluf is not a clown. In reality, he is the electrician, merely doubling as Patapluf.

Estrella's version of the authentic ending is not the conclusion of the play. César insists that the show must go on. They return once again to the moment when the train is about to leave that will take César away with Laura, thus abandoning Estrella. This time César and Estrella enact the illusion that we had previously anticipated as reality. In order to remain with the woman he loves César lets Laura go off by herself; he and Estrella will live happily ever after. Offering the hope that the illusion may become reality, that the line between theater and life may disappear, Estrella tells the audience: "Who knows, ladies and gentlemen, if by dint of pretending it night and day we will not someday really come to love each other" (V, 487). As the curtain closes, Salom's metaphorical trapeze is on the upswing; the audience is free to interpret the ending as a potentially happy one in spite of Estrella's earlier pronouncement.

For Pirandello, truth is never absolute. Each individual has his or her own relative truth, which may be a deliberately assumed illusion. Characters become the masks they wear, thus losing their true identities. Salom's treatment of the illusion-reality theme in *Trip on a Trapeze* is to a large extent Pirandellian. Estrella and Patapluf have diametrically opposed views of Plim. Similarly, she and César have very different opinions of Laura, but Laura is presented only through Estrella's interpretation of her. The real Laura never appears. César objects that Estrella's portrayal of Laura is false, just as Estrella later objects that the ending César wishes to stage is a lie. There are levels of fiction even within César and Estrella's portrayal of themselves. If the image they project of themselves in the past is a fictionalized one, how may one know if the portrayal of themselves in the present is the truth or merely another mask?

The planes of reality as well as the role-playing in Salom's theatrical game are presented in multiple layers. Within her role as herself at eighteen, Estrella creates for César the illusion that she is a sexually experienced forty-year-old so that he may become her lover without feeling guilty. Within her role as Laura, she plays a scene in which she displays great affection for César—only to reveal that the scene is just that, a rehearsal for a new circus act. César as Schmitt becomes a policeman who both threatens to arrest Estrella for stealing Patapluf's dog and tries to buy her sexual favors.[18] The result is a Chinese puzzle in which the characters create an illusion-within-an-illusion-within-an-illusion. The transition between different characters is handled with minimal costume changes. Estrella becomes Laura by donning a blond wig; César becomes Schmitt by putting on a moustache and smoking a cigar. The transitions between the different masks of the same character are more subtle, thus reinforcing the Pirandellian ambiguity.

Salom uses a number of devices to destroy the illusionism of the play. The audience is constantly reminded that what they are witnessing is theater. The characters address the audience directly, protesting that what they are staging is not true. Estrella in particular interrupts the action in this manner, but she emphasizes theatricalism in other ways as well. Conscious that she is playing a role, she characterizes herself as the ingenue: "I am young, innocent, good, patient and candid, as every female protagonist should be" (V, 452). Near the end of the first act, when Estrella has succeeded in preventing the brokenhearted César from committing suicide and their happiness together seems possible, she wishes to stop the action: "Curtain, curtain, curtain! Stories ought to end at just the right moment. It's a shame that, as in life, they have to go on" (V, 444). As the second act begins, she stops the curtain at the halfway point, protesting against the role she is obliged to play over and over (V, 447). She would prefer to rewrite the script. Momentarily casting herself in the role of stage manager, she later tells Plim that there will be soft music, strange lighting, and that César will be in love with her (V, 462). She succeeds in evoking the special effects, but she cannot change the story.

Applying the same impressionistic staging techniques that contributed to the success of *The Trunk of Disguises*, Salom introduces various moments of pantomime. To create the circus itself, César juggles imaginary balls and walks an imaginary tightrope; Laura tames an imaginary lion. The train, which forms an important element in the plot, is evoked first by sound effects and then, in the final scene, by the actors. Estrella climbs on Cesar's shoulders;[19] he imitates the motion of the train while she creates the appropriate noises.

Trip on a Trapeze, as a theatrical game, incorporates an obvious playfulness into its staging and characterizations. In act 1, Laura performs a feat of magic by transforming César into a parrot. When César attempts suicide, the rope Estrella gives him is several times too long; he naturally lands on his feet. The poison he then tries is really crème de menthe; he becomes drunk and begins to see everything in a bright green light, a color that traditionally symbolizes hope. The allegedly dead Estrella appears to him on the trapeze under that same colored light. César's inebriation as well as his confusion the next morning is treated on a farcical level. Similarly, the characterizations, particularly those of Schmitt, Laura, and Patapluf, are in fact caricatures, the stock types associated with farce. César and Estrella in their moments of anguish sometimes transcend farce, but their role-playing also invariably returns to the exaggerated style of low comedy. The result is a kind of distancing that keeps the audience from identifying too closely with the characters. The action swings between the potentially tragic and the obviously comic, between a serious comment on the human condition and the farcical tone found in various scenes throughout Salom's plays of poetic fantasy.

Chronologically, *The Trunk of Disguises*, the two versions of *Parcheesi Party*, and *Trip on a Trapeze* fall within the period of Salom's serious, moralistic plays. The works of poetic fantasy do not represent the dominant trend in his theater of the 1960s, yet they are significant not only for their individual literary merit but also for their innovative staging. They reflect Salom's increasing skill as a theatrical craftsman, thus serving as important preparation for his mature plays of the 1970s.

CHAPTER 6

More Morality Plays

THROUGHOUT most of his career as a playwright, Salom has shown a marked interest in moralistic theater. Many of his plays, published and unpublished, from *Mama's Smiling* through the decade of the 1960s, are intended to teach a moral or religious lesson. Such is the case of the four Inspector Ruiz plays analyzed in chapter 3 as well as two of the three early comedies studied in chapter 4. In spite of the wide variation in their themes and settings, three other dramas staged between 1965 and 1970 continue to evince this tendency. *Mirror for Two Women* is thematically related to the dramas of guilt and remorse and, like them, reflects the influence of J. B. Priestley. *The House of the "Chivas,"* Salom's most successful play to date and his only one to deal with the Civil War, once again presents a protagonist who rejects love to remain faithful to his religious and moral values. *The Empty Beach*, reminiscent of medieval morality plays, is a religious allegory whose characters represent life, physical pleasure, death, and God.

I Espejo para dos mujeres

Staged in both Barcelona and Madrid in the fall of 1965, *Espejo para dos mujeres* [Mirror for Two Women] is one of the three relative failures that followed the triumph of *The Trunk of Disguises*. Very different from the latter in structure and tone, *Mirror for Two Women* represents a return both to the kind of didactic drama that characterized Salom's earlier theatrical efforts and to conventional realism. While it is neither so militantly Catholic nor so excessively melodramatic as *The Fourth Player*, its theme is clearly religious and its ending is almost identical to that of *The Message*. Salom recalls that *Mirror for Two Women* was influenced in broad terms by Priestley's *Eden End* and rather more indirectly by Anton Chekhov, a playwright to whom Priestley also acknowledged a certain debt.[1] Both

Eden End and *Mirror for Two Women* utilize single stage settings representing respectable sitting rooms; time is linear.

The basic story of the two dramas might be called "the prodigal daughter." In the English play, Stella had run away from home to become an actress. When she returns after an absence of six years, she is welcomed back by all except her younger sister Lilian, who has always resented the favoritism shown Stella and now sees in her a rival for the man she loves. In Stella's absence, the family created the illusion that she enjoys a successful career on the stage; in truth she has failed and the actor she married is an alcoholic. Given Lilian's hostility and the reality of her own life, Stella realizes that to remain in the family home which she sought as a refuge will precipitate her sick father's death. She sacrifices her own possibility of happiness by leaving, thus maintaining her father's belief in her.

Although Salom's plot differs from Priestley's in a number of ways, his story, too, revolves around the return of a prodigal daughter, a love conflict between the two sisters, and a personal sacrifice by one of them. In the Spanish drama, Tina had left her conservative Catholic home ten years earlier to marry a French atheist. Her father, who never forgave her, is now dead. Elegant and sophisticated, she presents a vivid contrast to her younger sister Laura when she returns to the provincial city in northern Spain following her husband's death. Unlike Priestley's Lilian, the virtuous Laura welcomes Tina back with open arms, even when she has cause for resentment. The women's group at the church, ignoring Laura's years of humble service, nominates the newly returned Tina to be their vice-president. Patricia, a longtime family servant who never appears on stage, is dying; she treats Laura harshly, even though the younger sister has patiently cared for her throughout her long illness, and shows affection only for Tina, who is as indifferent to her as she is to the religious and moral values for which Laura stands.

Just as Stella's family in *Eden End* had created an illusion about the absent daughter, Laura has always assumed that Tina had married for love and had found happiness. In truth, Tina had been encouraged by her cynical husband to seek satisfaction in extramarital affairs. Her latest lover, Peter, has accompanied her to Spain. Ten years younger than Tina, Peter is supported by her. When he meets Laura, he is reminded of his own younger sister, who is similarly innocent and religious. He falls in love with Laura, even though he continues his affair with Tina. As the plot develops, Laura is gradually disabused of her illusions. Peter tells her of Tina's infidelity. Suspecting Laura's interest in Peter, Tina responds with jealousy, informing her naive younger sister that Peter himself is her current lover. Later, when she has been drinking, Tina decides to explain the dying Patricia's aversion to Laura and to religion. Before Laura was born, Patricia had been seduced by their supposedly pious father; when she had become pregnant, he had forced her to have an abortion. It was Patricia's story that strengthened Tina's resolve to leave home and marry contrary to her father's wishes.

Strong in her religious faith and in her faith in others, Laura's reaction to the sad truths is marked by Christian charity. She is convinced that her father might have been weak but that he was not cynical or hypocritical. She urges Tina to persuade Patricia to allow the priest to come and to receive the last rites. She is sure that Tina herself can be saved: "All that you believed as a little girl is not dead. There is still something in you capable of being reborn some day!"[2] Because of Laura's influence, Peter decides not to go back to France with Tina but rather to return to his own home and begin his life over. He asks Laura to go with him to America and marry him. Laura loves Peter, but she believes it is her duty to remain where she is, make a home for Tina, and be loyal to her sister. She tells Peter, "Poor Patricia, because she hated my father, hated God. Tina would hate me and God has brought her to me here so that I can help her. That is much more important than what you call my little share of happiness" (*M*, 55). In the final scene, Peter is calling Laura from the airport, but she merely lets the phone ring, allowing him to go away without her.

The essential difference between the Priestley play and *Mirror for Two Women* lies in Laura's religious conviction. Unlike Lilian, who cannot respond charitably to the returning prodigal, Laura considers no sacrifice too great to provide a refuge for her sister from the harsh realities of a materialistic world. Priestley's Stella cannot go home again; symbolically, her family's country estate is called Eden End. Similarly, in Chekhov's plays, the new order—that of the modern, materialistic world—invariably supplants the old order and the old values. Salom in the early 1960s still believed that the old order and the old values could and would triumph. Patricia may die without confessing to the priest, but there is at least some hope that God will have forgiven her. Peter and Tina appear to be saved by Laura's faith, and Laura herself will remain at her post, finding fulfillment in following her conscience and her moral duty.

In *Mirror for Two Women* Salom, the moralist, questions the meaning of life. Tina characterizes her younger sister as someone who

"has passed through life without grazing it, without living it" (*M*, 21).
In proposing to her, Peter tells Laura that she cannot renounce life,
that she must live it (*M*, 54). The play's message, however, is that only
through renunciation comes true happiness. Like Flora at the conclusion of *The Message*, Laura steels herself against momentary temptation, placing duty and loyalty above love. Adrián of *Lack of Evidence*
and *The Night of the Hundred Birds*, lacking Laura's strength of
character, had yielded to temptation with resultant tragedy. Characters like Adrián, Tina, and Peter have mistaken superficial excite-
ment for life, but virtuous people like Laura and Adrián's wife Juana,
who appear to the others to lead gray existences, are, in fact, the ones
who have found the true path. Love may best be expressed not
through sexual gratification but through personal sacrifice.

Mirror for Two Women is defective in several ways. Like *The
Message*, it is a "well-made play" whose plot development seems
contrived. In the opening scene, no sooner does Laura mention to
her friend Rosa that Tina may be returning from France than Tina
herself arrives at the door. In the second act, Peter lets himself in the
house with his own key and unburdens his soul to Tina through her
bedroom door, only to have Laura emerge from the room. Because
Salom's intention is didactic, the characterizations also seem contrived. It is difficult to believe that Tina would voluntarily return to a
small, conservative city with her portable bar and her clandestine
lover and even more difficult to believe that the church women would
accept her or that Laura would not know that Peter enters the house
each night. In *The Night of the Hundred Birds* Adrián's realization
that he should have preferred the virtuous Juana to the immoral
Lilian is credible. In *Mirror for Two Women* Peter's rejection of Tina
in favor of Laura after seeing the latter asleep on the couch in her
bathrobe and hairnet is much harder to accept. The result is a play
that verges on melodrama because Salom has subordinated the
psychological development of his characters to his moral intent.

II   La casa de las Chivas

Underlying *La casa de las Chivas* [The House of the "Chivas"] is
the same dichotomy between renunciation and an erroneous understanding of life that forms the basic theme of *Mirror for Two Women*.
Nevertheless, while the latter drama elicited mixed reactions and has
been labeled conventional, false, and uneven,[3] *The House of the
"Chivas"* has proved to be Salom's most successful play to date and

one of the most successful in the contemporary Spanish theater. To what may one ascribe its enormous popularity? The playwright, who personally does not consider the work to be one of his best and now rejects the moralistic attitude of the principal male character, attributes its appeal to two elements: the background of the Civil War and the realistic characterizations.[4]

By the late 1960s, writers in Spain were finally able to treat the Civil War objectively. Whereas earlier literary works tended to portray the strife from the perspective of the winning side, with a concomitant negative view of the Republicans, gradually the one-sided presentation yielded to a more objective analysis and then to a demythification of the war. The change came in the novel first,[5] then in the theater. On the Madrid stage, Antonio Buero Vallejo's *El tragaluz* [The Basement Window] and Antonio Gala's *Noviembre y un poco de yerba* [November and a Little Grass], both produced in 1967, dealt with the conflict tangentially by depicting its lingering aftermath, but Salom asserts that his drama was the first to show the war itself from the Republican side. The playwright's intent is not political; his emphasis is on the human dimension. The result, as one critic in Barcelona noted, is somewhat paradoxical: "Until now the theme of the Civil War had not been shown in the theater with such dispassionate and yet passionate objectivity."[6] The particular blend of background and focus was a compelling one for the Spanish audience, and, according to Marqueríe, the basis for the play's record-breaking run: ". . . it is the contemporary Spanish realistic drama in which a testimonial and objective vision of the enormous moral and physical trauma of our war is combined with a religious preoccupation" (191). The moral struggle of individual characters, which tends to be artificial and hence melodramatic in Salom's earlier works, gains in verisimilitude when played against the backdrop of a cataclysm.

The single stage setting for Salom's drama is a house behind the front lines in the Republican zone of eastern Spain; the action begins in the summer of 1938 and continues, in an episodic structure, over a period of time into the final months of the war when the Nationalist victory is inevitable. The playwright presents the story as being one that really happened. In his self-criticism, he states that the house of the "Chivas" still stands within a hundred kilometers of Barcelona.[7] In the closing moments of the play, one of the actors addresses the audience, assuring them that the story is completely true and informing them what happened to the principal survivors.[8] Alvaro is quite correct in observing that this possible historical reality is far less important than dramatic reality. Perhaps nine people really did experience the war together in such a house, but more importantly, "even if the play were pure invention, they interest us and move us as dramatic characters."[9]

These characters, brought together by chance because of the war, include three civilians—a father and his two daughters—and six soldiers. Although other civilians have fled the war zone, the father has stubbornly and childishly remained, clinging to the house and land that represent a lifetime of savings and work. He is unwilling or unable to grasp the reality of their situation, and it is the older daughter, Petra, who takes command. In exchange for her sexual favors and her housework, Petra receives enough food from the soldiers to keep the family alive. By gratifying the men's desires and by isolating her father and the adolescent Trini in the attic, Petra also attempts to protect the young girl's virtue and the old man's illusions about his own authority and about Petra's life.

As a group, the soldiers react to the dangers of war and the uncertainty of the future by seeking pleasure where they may find it. Their actions and words are marked by a crude realism in keeping with the circumstances. Salom is careful to individualize them, however, avoiding stereotypical images of totally depraved or brutalized men; as the play progresses, they are each seen to be complex human beings. Five of the men—the sergeant Mariano, Villalba, Guzmán, *Sopla*, and *Nene*—have been living in the house for several weeks when the play begins. Mariano appears to be the only one with a military orientation or any strong self-identification with the liberal, anticlerical cause; early in the play he announces that the two things he most abhors in life are deserters and priests (*H*, 172). He is also the only one to pursue Trini. Even Guzmán, who is the coarsest in his treatment of Petra, is willing to respect the teenager. Villalba and *Sopla*, like the other two, are mature men who share Petra's services. *Nene*, on the other hand, as his nickname indicates, is just a kid; *Sopla* and Guzmán are distressed that the shy boy is still a virgin. Villalba, who is seen as the most humane and sensitive of the older men, identifies the adolescent with his own oldest son and attempts, however weakly, to intervene on his behalf.

Sharply distinguished from these five soldiers by his level of education and by his spirituality is Juan, the colonel's chauffeur who arrives as a new lodger, bringing with him a suitcase of philosophy books and a package of food from France. The soldiers respond to Juan with attitudes ranging from mild suspicion to Mariano's open hostility; but Petra is immediately impressed by his courtesy and generosity, and Trini soon falls in love with him. Although to a large extent *The House of the "Chivas"* is a collective drama without a single protagonist, the central action of the play revolves around Juan and Trini. Feeling that he has a calling to be a priest, Juan rejects the young girl's love. In retaliation, she gives herself to Mariano, even though she knows that the middle-aged sergeant is a married man with children. Ultimately her unrequited love leads her to drive deliberately into an ambush, thus in effect committing suicide.

From the opening minutes of the play, Salom makes it clear that his characters are radically and consistently affected by the war. Hunger, fear, uncertainty, and loneliness are the motivating factors in their existences. Faced with the threat of death, traditional values lose their meaning. Even the relatively humane Villalba rejoices at the death of two officers because he is able to claim their rations as booty. Sex becomes a means of momentary escape from an unacceptable reality. Guzmán seems to have led a depraved existence before joining the army, but Mariano and Villalba are family men. Alonso, a soldier killed while trying to desert, has left behind a photo of his wife and baby and a religious picture. *Nene,* who misses his fifteen-year-old girl friend, wears a religious medal that she gave him. Petra is the daughter of a prostitute—the notorious *Chiva* who abandoned her family when Trini was an infant—but it is unclear when and why she became a prostitute herself; certainly it is obvious that she now sells herself primarily from necessity.[10] In a world turned upside down, it is easy for individuals to lose their sense of direction. At heart *Nene* wants to remain faithful to his sweetheart and his concepts of right and wrong, but he allows *Sopla* to buy from Petra his initiation into manhood. Although he knows that Trini still loves Juan, Mariano decides to abandon his wife and family for the young girl; it is an anguished attempt to set aside the past and start a new life. Trini, fearful that she may die before she really lives, confuses life with physical love. Only Juan, with his deep and abiding faith in God, is able to transcend momentary despair and temptation.

The horror and misery of war lead to a loss in traditional values but do not totally erase a sense of humanity. Mariano is sometimes a violent and brutal man, but, as Juan tells him, "You are better than you think" (*H*, 234); he cannot kill Juan or anyone else in cold blood. He also cannot forsake either his cause or the young girl he has seduced. Guzmán, whom Petra accuses of having been a pimp, goes out of his way to visit Mariano's family and bring news of them to the absent soldier. When the wounded Villalba wants to go home, *Sopla* agrees to risk his own life to try to take him there. Even though death is commonplace, comradeship is still important. Except for Mariano, the other soldiers are noticeably affected by the deaths of Alonso and *Nene*. Petra, the fallen woman, finds in the tragedy of the war the strength of character necessary to redeem herself.

In *The House of the "Chivas"*, none of the characters is two dimensional. Directly or indirectly they are made to reveal inner conflicts and deep emotions. In the case of the principal figures, not only their individual psychological development but also their interaction is shown to be complex.[11] Juan is in a pivotal position with respect to both sisters; to some extent, he is the catalyst for Trini's destruction and Petra's salvation. His responsibility is only a limited one, however. Trini begins to rebel against Petra's protectiveness before his arrival, and Petra has yearned for some time to change her own life. Her desire to redeem herself and to seek some deeper meaning to life is apparent from the beginning of the drama. She is ferocious in her efforts to keep Trini from falling into the path of immorality that she and their mother have followed. She considers her own promiscuity to be wrong and would like to believe that she could start over. In a dialogue with her father, she asks about *Chiva* and disagrees with him when he says such a woman can never reform: "A woman can marry and begin again as if she were a young girl. . . . One can always change" (*H*, 178). She recognizes Juan's moral superiority and is attracted to him because of it. While the soldiers may believe that Juan rejects Trini because he is homosexual, Petra knows that he is a normal man with normal desires. Finding in Juan the spiritual guide that she has previously lacked, she seeks from him the assurance her father had denied her that she can change her life. Juan speaks to her of God's forgiveness and of his own faith, a faith that Petra would like to share: "Life cannot be only this, so petty, so boring, so monotonous. . . . Perhaps if I believed, I would be happier, even if in the end it all turned out to be a lie. I don't know, I don't know . . ." (*H*, 211).

Realistically, Petra's conversion is not instantaneous. In spite of her yearning to be good and her awareness that *Nene* is an innocent and idealistic boy, she accepts *Sopla*'s payment to sleep with the young man. In fact, as she later tells Juan, it is precisely because *Nene* is shy and innocent that she cooperates: "I hoped to find all that I had lost. As if my body, upon contact with his, would be virgin again . . ." (*H*, 227). In this respect, the attraction she feels for *Nene* is analogous to Mariano's attachment to Trini. Petra, however, finds not vicarious youth and innocence but rather an overwhelming burden of guilt and shame. The boy's remorse after their lovemaking is all too apparent; he cries himself to sleep. The next morning he is killed during a bombing attack. The anguished Petra is impelled to confess her sins to Juan, and, forcing him into assuming the role of a priest, begs his absolution. Her conversion is now complete. Petra will dedicate herself in the years to come. to caring for her father and her lost mother, whom she finds in a hospital during the last months of the war. Redemption is possible for both "Chivas."

In contrast with Petra's anguished search for a new beginning is Trini's impatience to taste the pleasures of life. The father may not perceive what is happening in his house, but Trini is fully conscious of her sister's activities with the soldiers. Typically adolescent, she is resentful of Petra's protectiveness and determined to explore life for herself. At night she hears laughter and music downstairs; she mistakenly believes that Petra thrives on the adulation of the men and merely wants to maintain her status as "queen of the chicken coop" (*H*, 158). While *Nene* is apparently deterred from sinking to the prevailing level of moral decadence by his previous religious training, Trini has no clear concept of right and wrong to guide her. Flattered by the attention Mariano has paid her and determined to defy Petra's authority, she leaves the attic to join what she believes to be an exciting party. Her rebellion and Juan's arrival coincide; her choice of him as the object of her love is immediate and natural.[12] She sees in him her chance for happinesss: "I know how to be happy. . . . Being loved by the man I love" (*H*, 184). Juan's response is incomprehensible to her: "There is only one Being who can really give that happiness, and only through renunciation is there a possibility of finding it" (*H*, 184). From Trini's limited perspective, life, love, and sex are synonymous terms. She offers Juan her body; when he refuses her, she accepts Mariano as her lover out of spite.

From her contact with Juan, Trini gains no understanding of his moral preoccupations, but she does come to realize that real love is more than physical lovemaking. Mariano is able to provide her with the sexual initiation that she had assumed to be life's big secret, but her unfulfilled love for Juan dominates her. When it appears that he has been killed in the bombing, she is beside herself with grief. At the end of the drama, after she has been separated from him for several months and is visibly pregnant, it is still Juan's love that she seeks. She now knows from Petra about Juan's religious vocation, but her love for him is unchanged. She is not willing to follow the advice given her by her sister and by Juan to renounce Mariano, but if Juan had returned her love, if the baby were his, not Mariano's, she would be content even if left alone: "I would feel myself sheltered by your memory and by your child" (*H*, 237). For her, Juan is the only possible path to happiness. Juan, however, cannot respond to that love: "I shall pray for you all of the days of my life. . . . That's all I can do" (*H*, 238). Rejected once again by Juan, unsure of her future with Mariano but determined not to become another *Chiva*, Trini decides to kill herself.

Although the inner conflicts of Petra and Trini eventually surface and are verbalized, Juan's deepest feelings remain ambiguous. On one level he is clearly an inner-directed person who can transcend the horror of the war through his faith. But on another level, at least partially concealed from view, he is a man struggling against his own passions. Shortly after his arrival, Petra warns Trini against falling in love with Juan. "You will never mean anything to him. . . . Neither we nor the war nor even death seem to matter very much to him as if he knew the secret of everything . . ." (*H*, 179–80). Juan appears sure of himself and secure in his faith when he talks to Petra of God, to Trini of the happiness that comes from renunciation, or to *Nene* of the meaning of manhood: "To be a man is to be one's own master" (*H*, 206). But Juan is not always in control. Particularly when he is exhausted, he must struggle against temptation. When Trini tries to seduce him, late one night, he momentarily succumbs and begins to caress her. When *Sopla* insinuates that he is a homosexual, Juan almost chokes the soldier to death. He is similarly tempted to respond to Mariano's hostility with physical aggression. These moments of weakness are only the outer manifestation of a continuing inner struggle. Juan receives daily letters of guidance from an old priest, now in hiding. Petra sees the old man with him one day in a café and correctly guesses that she is witnessing a confession.[13] "I suppose you asked him to come to town to give you a hand. . . . I thought probably because of Trini." "It's possible," Juan replies (*H*, 209). The implication is that Juan is attracted to Trini and that his lack of response to her love is a facade. Although his answers to her about his feelings are always the correct ones for a future priest, there are moments when he appears to affect his attitude and others when he is visibly shaken by her involvement with Mariano, her pregnancy, and her death. The critical opinion that Juan maintains his purity "without great effort" is undoubtedly an erroneous one.[14]

Juan also doubts the correctness from a religious point of view of the positions he has taken vis-à-vis the other characters. After hearing Petra's confession of guilt, he questions his role: "It may be, at heart, that I am responsible for all this—for having not made you understand God's reasons. . . . While I was defending His Law, perhaps I forgot the other, that of charity" (*H,* 228). In this vein, Fernando Díaz-Plaja has suggested that a more mature and experienced priest "would have resolved the conflict in another way" (Marquerie, 183). Salom himself, from the perspective of the present, has completely rejected his character's intransigence.[15] How Juan might have appeased Trini and prevented her from following the course of action that she does without giving up his religious vocation is, however, not clear. The dramatic force of the play undoubtedly resides in the lack of easy solutions to the inner conflicts of the various characters.

The initial success of *The House of the "Chivas"* may be attributed in part to its then daring treatment of the Civil War, but its continued popularity, including that of foreign productions and of the television play in 1978, indicates that its appeal is much more universal. Frequently compared to the works of Graham Greene, it is a Catholic drama dealing with questions of sin and salvation.[16] The characters, caught in a brutal reality and torn by their passions and fears, are seen as real human beings striving desperately for some form of happiness—perhaps love, perhaps spiritual redemption. Avoiding the didactic tone of some of his earlier moralistic plays, developing his plot and characters more carefully so that their actions seem more natural and less melodramatic, Salom has achieved here his work of greatest dramatic intensity.

III   La playa vacía

When *La playa vacía* [The Empty Beach] opened in Madrid in November, 1970, *The House of the "Chivas"* had just finished its triumphant run in the capital the preceding month. Several years separate the composition of the plays, however, and, in spite of their common emphasis on religious themes, they are substantially differ-

ent in form and intent. An allegory utilizing certain theatricalist
techniques, *The Empty Beach* is more closely related to the plays of
poetic fantasy, particularly *The Trunk of Disguises*, in its staging and
characterization than to the conventional realism of the Civil War
drama. Moreover, the later play reveals Salom's changing philosophy
of life. Gone is the moralistic approach to guilt and remorse, renunciation and redemption. Eschewing his previous rigid stance, Salom
ceases to pass judgment, preferring instead merely to present the
human condition with compassion.

The setting for Salom's allegory is an isolated summer resort in late
autumn, just as the last tourists depart. Victoria, the owner, is a
middle-aged widow who, now that her old companion Sofía has died,
taking with her many of Victoria's memories, faces the prospect of a
solitary winter. She urges Pablo, the young man in charge of the
beach equipment, to remain with her. Despite her claims that, unlike
the foreign women who have paid Pablo well for his services, her
interest in him is not sexual, ultimately they agree that he will stay
and gratify her desires as long as her money lasts.

Although Victoria and Pablo are initially both presented as real
people rather than purely allegorical figures, Salom makes his symbolic intent clear from the opening scene. The annual departure of
the German and French tourists from the Spanish beaches has its
basis in contemporary reality; the existence of Spanish male prostitutes since the onslaught of the tourist wave in the 1960s has been
pointed out with some frequency in the novel.[17] But the empty beach
and Pablo's sexual liaisons transcend the sociological. Pablo believes
that women want him only for physical pleasure; Victoria is sure that
they are trying to escape momentarily from their solitude. For her,
everyone has an empty beach from which to flee.[18] Through Pablo,
Victoria is seeking release both from loneliness and from her fear of
death. She prefers to say that Sofía has gone away, even avoiding the
use of the verb "to die." She still hopes that a couple who disappeared
at sea on a paddle boat early in the summer will miraculously reap-
pear alive. On an empty beach facing the endless expanse of water,
she finds that her anguish is intensified: "Few human beings can
confront alone 360° of truth," she tells Pablo, "I can't, I certainly
can't" (*E*, 327). It is to escape the truth of impending death that
Victoria, whose greatest love is life, needs the companionship of
Pablo, the representative of pleasure.[19]

In the second scene,[20] the symbolic intent of *The Empty Beach* is
reinforced by the arrival of two mysterious characters—Tana, a young

woman whose apparently lifeless form floats in on a log, and Don, an elderly shopkeeper who also serves as letter carrier, messenger, deliveryman, and mechanic. Although their true identities are not directly expressed, there is no doubt as to the allegorical nature of these figures: Tana is Thanatos (Death) and Don is Dominus (God). The drama that ensues is largely the inner struggle of Victoria as she allies herself now with Pablo, now with Don, in her effort to resist Tana, who both repels her and comforts her. In the end, Pablo, who has been drugged by Tana, can be nothing but a memory for Victoria; calling for Don, who has promised to be always at her side, Victoria willingly drifts out to sea on the same paddle boat that had months before taken the missing couple to their deaths.

Salom's message in *The Empty Beach* is overtly metaphysical. He wishes to explore the meaning of life and death, the longing for (but limitations of) physical pleasure as a means of escaping from existential anguish, the continuing significance of God even in a world that has decreed Him to be dead. While his use of allegory clearly links the work to the medieval morality play or the Golden Age *auto sacramental*, Salom's development of his individual characters and their interrelationships is more complex and of greater dramatic interest.[21]

Neither Victoria nor Pablo realize who Tana is when she first arrives; the revelation is hence a gradual process both for them and for the audience. Even as she becomes aware that Tana is Death, Victoria vacillates in determining what course of action she should follow. Pablo, too, is fascinated by Tana, although Tana's interest is Victoria (Life), not Pablo (Pleasure). It is only when faced with death that Victoria comes to know Don, whose patience and understanding are infinite. If in Salom's earlier, more didactic plays, it was necessary for his characters to renounce life and pleasure in order to seek spiritual salvation, from his perspective in 1970 such renunciation is no longer obligatory. Pablo openly rejects Don, criticizing both his silence and his tendency to sit in judgment at inopportune times, but Don does not condemn pleasure, only the potential loss of free will for those who let pleasure dominate them: "I don't hate you. Why should I? On the contrary, I have nothing against you. But I don't like to see one person enslaved by another . . ." (*E*, 373). Victoria, who could not decide to leave Pablo to go with Don, nevertheless calls to him when she drifts out to sea. That is enough to guarantee her redemption; in the final scene, when the arrival of spring brings with it the returning tourists, Don is there to retrieve Victoria's body from the water: "She went seeking me before. It is just that we finally find one another and that I take her where she wanted to go" (*E*, 399).

Salom's religious beliefs are obviously no longer rooted in the rigid Catholic doctrine that he previously advocated. As a result he not only emphasizes a forgiving and compassionate God but also achieves a greater universality as he focuses more generally on the human condition. Victoria's struggle is that of every person. Like Sofía before her, she finds comfort in contact with Don and regrets that she did not come to know him sooner: "You are a great guy, Don. I don't understand how I overlooked you so long . . ." (*E*, 366). God can provide the necessary support to make life on the empty beach tolerable. His sheltering presence continues even beyond death. But God cannot protect one from death; indeed, it is Don who delivers to Tana the names of those she is to claim. If Victoria has been unaware of Don's existence, Tana is at once familiar to her: "I am sure that I have had her always at my side since I was born. That she has accompanied me everywhere and watched over my sleep at night" (*E*, 371). Like the Roman philosopher Seneca, Salom perceives dying as a process that begins from the moment of birth.[22] Tana has always been with Victoria as she has been with those who have already died: Victoria's husband, Sofía, the couple who disappeared on the paddle boat. As the play ends and the boatload of tourists approaches, Don hands Tana a letter with the name Ronald, repeating an earlier scene when he had assigned Victoria to her. The structure of the play is circular, reinforcing the inevitable life-death cycle of human existence.[23]

While *The Empty Beach* is interesting as a reflection of Salom's own evolving philosophy and of contemporary theology, what most distinguishes the play is its use of innovative staging devices. Lorenzo López Sancho is correct in rejecting the frequent comparison of the Catalan's allegory with Alejandro Casona's *La dama del alba* [The Lady of the Dawn] staged in Buenos Aires in 1944, and in Madrid in 1962.[24] The differences lie not only in the portrayal of death, as the critic notes, but even more obviously in the approach to theater. Casona's play transcends realism primarily through the introduction of the supernatural and of elements of folklore; the staging itself is quite consistent with conventional realism. On the other hand, Salom, who does not cloak death in a poetic idealization like Casona, does develop his extended metaphor of existential anguish within the current of nonrepresentational theater.

Basic to the setting of *The Empty Beach* is the sea, symbol of both life and death. The sea brings the boatloads of tourists—Victoria's main contact with the outer world—as well as Tana's log and the fatal paddleboat. None of these elements ever appear on stage.[25] The beach is created by sand extending onto the apron; it is up to the actors, primarily Pablo, to evoke for the audience the sea, the departing and arriving tourists, and the floating objects. Like the imaginary train in *The Trunk of Disguises*, the boat exists only through the sound of the motor and Pablo's one-sided conversation with the passengers. Because the sea is presumably the auditorium, the audience is obliged to enter immediately into the theatrical fantasy. In the Madrid production, to retrieve Tana's body from the water, Pablo carries her through the audience up to the stage.

As was true in the plays of poetic fantasy but to a much lesser extent, Salom introduces songs and poetry.[26] Pablo establishes his hedonistic philosophy with an almost identical song and dance at the beginning and the end of the drama. Don, immediately after the arrival of Tana, recites a poem—ostensibly a scene from a play in which Victoria had appeared during her early career as an actress—in which he announces that death has arrived. These three moments are intended to establish and reinforce the play's symbolic level. The use of doubling and disguises serves a similar function. Through these devices Victoria, like Juan in *The Trunk of Disguises*, is able to relive significant episodes from her past as the action shifts to the plane of poetic fantasy.

The first reference to a fantasized past occurs in the second scene of the first act, even before the arrival of Tana and Don. In a dialogue with Pablo, Victoria questions whether or not he is real: "Perhaps you only exist here, in my imagination . . ." (*E*, 336–37). Implying that Pablo is indeed merely the manifestation of her subconscious, Victoria asserts that her parents and her grandfather, too, are alive, and that she is five years old: "A little girl, yes, why not? Me, me, me! Have they changed me? Have they given me other bones and flesh?" (*E*, 338). The concept is similar to that of *The Trunk of Disguises*; the person's past still lives in the present, at least in the individual's inner world. In her attempt to escape from the reality of death, Victoria seeks refuge alternately in pleasure and in the security of a distant childhood. The grandfather, who died in 1928, is a protective figure who shields the little girl from harm as she plays on the beach. Time has not passed. Victoria forces Pablo into assuming the attitude of the grandfather toward her—drying her feet and urging her to get out of her wet clothes—but the scene is not presented as a complete transition from one level of reality to another.

In the following scene, again repeating a device from *The Trunk of Disguises*, Tana appears with a box of costumes. Victoria first identifies the clothes as belonging to those who have died and then finds among them her first grown-up dress, which she puts on. With an appropriate change of lighting, the action shifts to an imaginary plane with Pablo and Tana doubling in the roles of the young Victoria's parents. Consistent with Salom's changing ideology and foreshadowing a related scene in *Lemon Peel*, the ensuing dialogue is a satire of "middle-class morality." The caricatured father and mother wish to keep their daughter from becoming an actress and force her instead into the kind of respectable marriage that family tradition requires: "A family like ours, whose women have always been deflowered by their husbands at 10:00 sharp on their wedding nights" (*E*, 359). The mother's adultery is of no consequence to the father provided that she maintain the proper appearance: "Goodby, dear. Until seven. Don't forget to change the sheets. I'm a man of honor" (*E*, 359). While Salom's social satire here is gratuitous and not clearly related to the main theme of the play, the arrival of Don brings the scene back to the symbolic level associated with the earlier reference to the past. Among the clothes in the box of disguises is a jacket belonging to Victoria's beloved grandfather. It not only fits Don but is identical to his own jacket. Metaphorically, God and the grandfather are one; separate from the hypocrisy and false morality represented by the parents, they are compassionate and loving figures who offer comfort and protection to the trusting child or the anguished adult.

In the second scene of the second act, a change in lighting again facilitates a transition to the imaginary plane of the past, this time with Tana doubling as Victoria's grandfather while Victoria assumes the role of herself as a little girl. The action shifts back and forth as Victoria violently rejects the substitution of Tana for the grandfather, thus returning the action to the present where she once more seeks refuge in Pablo before succumbing to death. Tana, in taking the grandfather's role, attempts to present herself as a benevolent figure, one who offers a kind of comfort and rest. While this image of death is not totally rejected, it is clear that Don, not Tana, fills the void for Victoria. As a child, she was not frightened by the sea if her grandfather was with her on the beach. Now calling upon Don, she is able to face the sea of death. Although Salom has softened his previous moralistic stance—accepting the pursuit of pleasure, including physical love, as an understandable human need—his basic interpretation of death and God is well within the Christian tradition.

In *The Empty Beach*, as in the plays of poetic fantasy, Salom juxtaposes two planes of reality. Various critics have found in this simultaneous treatment of the realistic and the symbolic either the drama's greatest strength or its greatest weakness.[27] Typical of the negative reaction is that of Carlos Luis Alvarez who feels that the two planes do not blend together properly because "they do not spring from the same dynamics."[28] In fact, they not only form a cohesive whole but may, in essence, form a single level of reality, that of Victoria's subconscious. As Manuel Rotellar has noted, the interest of the play rises from Salom's "having humanized the symbols, bringing them close to the spectator."[29] Nevertheless, Pablo, Tana, and Don are not real people; rather, they are the projections of Victoria's inner struggle.[30] They are universal symbols, a continuing part of human existence, and hence remain after Victoria is dead; but throughout much of the drama, they are seen as part of Victoria's psychological reality. The retreats to Victoria's past are clearly the externalization of her inner world, but even the plane of the present may be so viewed. Victoria explains the psychological symbolism of the empty beach on which she finds herself. It is at her request that Pablo is present; later she suggests that, in fact, he does not exist. She anticipates the arrival of Tana before the log appears on the horizon; but Tana has always been with her and is now within her. Don appears when Tana has become a physical presence; only gradually does Victoria realize that he is responding to her silent call. Whether one views the play as a juxtaposition of two distinct planes or varying levels of a single imaginary world, the symbolic and psychological elements are always there, never far beneath the surface action, thus creating a structural unity. With its allegorical form, *The Empty Beach* is the most overtly metaphysical of Salom's plays and the culmination of his religious theater. Paradoxically, it is a morality play without a rigid moral lesson. Salom no longer pretends to have absolute answers to the basic questions on the meaning of life and death.[31] As a result, he has avoided the pitfalls of his earlier moralistic melodramas and has achieved not only a more theatrical expression of his abiding concern for humanity but also his most universal statement on the need for religious faith.

CHAPTER 7

Plays of Political and Social Commentary

WITH the exception of the unpublished *Motor Running*, Salom's early plays avoided social and political themes while placing emphasis on religious and moral questions. Even *The House of the "Chivas,"* with its Civil War setting, is primarily a psychological and moral drama. By the end of the 1960s, however, the Catalan's theater began to reflect the evolution in his own personal ideology. *The Heirs Apparent* (1969), in showing the decline of a patriarchal industrialist family, makes an indirect commentary on the Franco regime. *Time of Swords* (1972), ostensibly a modernization of the Christ story, similarly carries a contemporary political message as does the historical farce *Nine Toasts for a King* (1974). *Lemon Peel* (1976), Salom's plea for divorce reform, includes a biting satire on various aspects of Spanish society. As a group, these works of political and social commentary represent the high point in Salom's theater to date.

I Los delfines

Winner of the Calderón de la Barca National Literature Prize, *Los delfines* [The Heirs Apparent] was staged in Barcelona in January, 1969, and in Madrid the following October by the National Theater Company of Barcelona. Like the two plays that immediately follow it in Salom's oeuvre, *The Empty Beach* and *Trip on a Trapeze*, it is a theatricalist work with an obvious level of symbolism. The setting designed by Sigfrido Burman for both productions emphasized these aspects of the play. A series of four platforms, connected by a spiral staircase and containing minimal furniture, facilitated fluidity in time and space; suspended from the railing of the stairs were numerous bicycles, tricycles, and wheels, symbolizing the childhood friendship and later separation by social class of Fernando Tuser, heir to the family industry, and Braulio, his servant.[1]

Described by the author as the protagonist-victim of the drama, Fernando is intended to represent the so-called "bridge generation."[2] The term has been widely used in Spain to refer to those who experienced the Civil War as children or adolescents; they are thus the link between their parents, who fought in the war, and their children, who have little interest in or sympathy with the old animosities.[3] Salom clearly views with compassion this middle generation whose education and environment guaranteed them to be "a mediocre people predestined for failure." In an interview preceding the premiere, Salom affirmed that the real victim of *The Heirs Apparent* was in fact his own generation, "joining hands with two strong, antagonistic, irreconcilable worlds, that of yesterday and that of tomorrow, an empty generation, one of transition that I fear is judged with undeserved severity, for as someone has said, it is unjust to judge individuals for the errors of their time."[4]

The action of the play begins on the evening of Juan Tuser's eightieth birthday party. The patriarch, who never appears on stage but whose domineering personality hovers ever in the background, dies before the party begins. Finding himself incapable of resolving the serious crises facing the company, Fernando seeks the help of Raúl, a former employee who has spent some years in the United States and has acquired expertise in modern technology and management. Raúl recommends vast changes, including giving up family control by selling stocks. Carolina, Fernando's mother, is determined to maintain the status quo. Caught between her active resistance to change and the disillusionment in his love affair with Susana—the daughter of Condomina, a loyal company man—Fernando commits suicide. Believing that she has won back control of the family business in spite of strikes threatened by the workers, Carolina attempts to move her grandson Fere into the position left vacant by his father. Fere, however, has long since rebelled against the company and all it stands for; as the play ends, he reiterates his intention of never acquiescing.

That *The Heirs Apparent* is an allegory is made clear from the opening lines of the play. Fernando, beginning to write a confession that will occupy him throughout the action, identifies himself and his father both as individuals and as representative figures. Juan Tuser is one of those who forged the prosperity of the country, one of those great men who sap the strength of the generation that follows: "One must have the force of a titan to fight against that. And I haven't had it . . . none of us has had it. They carefully educated us from childhood on so that we would not have it. We are the heirs, the dauphins of a world propped up on family names."[5] For Fernando, his father, who managed in spite of pain to put on his tuxedo before dying, was "the prototype of a generation that worshipped appearance" (D, 264).

Similarly, all of the other characters in the drama are representative figures. As Jaime Delgado has carefully pointed out, they may be divided not only into the three generations but also into differing attitudes and social classes within those groups (Delgado, xxxix–xlvi). Carolina stands alone as the survivor of the oldest generation, but she is supported in her inflexible defense of the past by the active collaboration of her daughter-in-law Luisa and by Condomina. Like the faithful servant Braulio, Condomina has always done as he was told and never questioned the judgment of a Tuser. Susana sees in both Braulio and her father innate strengths of character that were stifled because of Juan Tuser. Her father might have been a more brilliant man if he had followed his own ideas instead of accepting Tuser's as infallible (D, 267). In order to break away from Tuser's control, Raúl had been forced to leave Spain; in America he had been free to develop the progressive stance that might in fact save the Spanish industry from total disaster. In the youngest generation, each of Fernando and Luisa's three children and Susana have chosen different paths, but all of them reject the rigid social stratification and moral hypocrisy inculcated by Juan and Carolina.

In developing his allegory, Salom uses to full advantage the double meaning of the word "sociedad," which may signify either company or society in Spanish. Hence each reference to Tuser's company may simultaneously be interpreted as referring to Spain or to contemporary society in general. Carolina's words of praise for the family business are tinged with irony, for they parody the conservative platitudes of the Franco regime. According to her, Juan has given them all "a happy and united society, without secrets or problems, grateful and proud of bearing the name that he made great" (D, 261); "a prosperous society, perfectly structured, in full development" (D, 264). Increasingly convinced that Juan's legacy is one of bankruptcy and decay, Fernando, on the other hand, announces that it is a "dying society that has no salvation" (D, 275). He criticizes his mother's efforts to use religion to keep him from attempting reforms: "It's our greatest sin. Converting God into another company employee" (D, 277). Fere, even more disenchanted than his father, finds the decadence to be universal: "It is not just this enterprise, Papa, it's all of civilization that is living on credit at the brink of disintegration. You're not the only one who finds his inheritance to be nothing but an empty chest" (*D*, 278). Turning to the audience, he accuses them all of belonging to the consumer society, of being enslaved by their possessions.

In his self-criticism, Salom indicated quite directly that *The Heirs Apparent* was not written as realistic drama: "It will suffice to move from the personal-conflict-anecdote level to the social-cultural-political-religious one or that of so many contemporary human activities to give to the work the true universal meaning that the author intended."[6] In keeping with this purpose, the staging is nonrepresentational and the characters, with the possible exception of Fernando, are two-dimensional rather than fully delineated figures. The playwright's intention apparently was to create the stark atmosphere appropriate to tragedy, an intention underscored by Burman's setting and the costumes, which were done in shades of gray and black with only a few touches of yellow.[7] Marquerie's analysis of the drama is particularly relevant in this respect. Given its focus, "neither the setting nor the technique nor the rhythm of the play could be those of a realistic treatment." The use of monologue and the fluidity of time further reinforce the allegorical and symbolic background (Marquerie, 196–97).

To a large extent, the dialogue and action of the play are the projection of Fernando's thoughts, not the "real" communication and interaction of the characters. In his introspective scenes, Fernando views both himself and others as symbolic figures; in effect, he introduces them to the audience defined by his perception of their attitudes. It is in part for this reason that the secondary figures generally appear as archetypes and tend to be seen in stark, contrasting tones rather than in the subtle shadings of psychological drama. In the opening scene of the play, for example, Fernando is seated at a desk on the first platform while Carolina is above him on the fourth platform. Fernando's written confession takes the form of a monologue; his mother's speeches, while related in content to Fernando's, are not her half of a dialogue but rather appear to be Fernando's projection of what he believes his mother thinks. Somewhat later in the same act, Fernando has a similar interchange with Luisa, who is located on the third platform, but again there is no real dialogue. Fernando not only imagines his wife's words but similarly evokes an interrogation of his three children to explore their attitudes. In the early scenes of the first act, Salom alternates this plane of reality—Fernando's consciousness—with the real action in the present—the family reunion leading up to the disclosure of Juan Tuser's death—while differentiating between the two by appropriate changes in lighting. In one scene, however, the two planes are simultaneous. As Condomina in the present responds to the current economic crisis facing the company, Fernando evokes from the past the beginning of his love affair with Susana.

The second act begins, like the first, with alternating speeches between Fernando, still at work writing his confession, and Carolina. As Fernando recalls his childhood, Carolina recedes to the past and assumes the tone of the authoritarian mother speaking to the young child. Fernando also imagines the conflicting attitudes of his snobbish wife and his rebellious daughter Tina relative to the latter's impending marriage to a merchant seaman. Viewing Condomina and Raúl as opposing forces representing resistance to change and desire for reform, Fernando creates a dialogue between the two in which this dichotomy is clearly expressed. Fernando's confession, aside from giving rise to the various scenes in which his memories or interpretation of the others' feelings are acted out, also allows for a limited amount of direct narration.[8]

Salom's use of two planes of reality is one found earlier in his plays of poetic fantasy and in *Lack of Evidence* but also anticipates techniques the playwright will use in *The Night of the Hundred Birds* and *Lemon Peel,* two of his most important works. In particular, the externalization of one character's consciousness relates *The Heirs Apparent* not only with Salom's own later dramas but also with other Spanish plays staged in Madrid during the same theatrical season: Torcuato Luca de Tena's *Hay una luz sobre la cama* [There's a Light Over the Bed, September, 1969] and Antonio Buero Vallejo's *El sueño de la razón* [The Sleep of Reason, February, 1970].

Critical reaction to *The Heirs Apparent* was mixed. The reviews from Barcelona were highly favorable, as are the more thorough studies of Delgado and Marquerie, but other commentators attacked the drama on various grounds, including development of character, rhythm, choice of story, and theme. The characters were labeled "robots" and "too archetypical."[9] Given that Salom had already established himself as a playwright very capable of creating "authentic human beings," one critic found it surprising that he had turned to the "almost metaphysical" and had his characters express themselves "in monologues rather than dramatically."[10] Salom was accused of forgetting that theater is "staged action"; as a result, his play is nothing but a dramatic essay.[11] Undoubtedly for reasons of censorship, no critic identified the obvious parallels between Juan Tuser and Franco, but less understandable were some of the reactions to the surface anecdote and underlying themes. The drama was termed interesting for having brought to the stage a theme of "economic reality," but it was weakened because the workers' strikes could not be related to any recent historic event.[12] The theme unfortunately was "limited to the upper-middle-class industrialists of Barcelona" or, conversely, would have been more effective if Salom had limited himself to Catalan reality.[13] Salom's transition from moralistic psychological drama to plays of political and social commentary was either not understood or was openly rejected by many critics in Madrid.[14]

The Heirs Apparent can be interpreted as an allegory reflecting prophetically upon post-Franco Spain. With little effort, one can develop the parallels between Salom's fictional characters and the various attitudes that emerged subsequent to the dictator's death, ranging from the reactionary supporters of Franco (Carolina, Condomina, Luisa) to a rebellious younger generation (Fere, Mara, Tina) and including the returning exiles (Raúl). The playwright predicts quite accurately what the conflicts will be, but he leaves unresolved the outcome of the struggle between left and right. As the play ends, Carolina is just as convinced that she will succeed in bending Fere's will to her own as Fere is determined to resist; their statements come not in dialogue, but in the kind of juxtaposed monologues that defined the Carolina–Fernando relationship at the beginning.[15]

Although the parallels between the Tuser family and contemporary Spain are obvious, *The Heirs Apparent* transcends political allegory by presenting the anguished situation of Fernando in a tragic light. "In general *The Heirs Apparent* has the deliberate hierarchism of a Greek tragedy, where protagonists and antagonists occupy fixed, ritualistic positions, but to that hierarchism is added, when appropriate, some suggestions of movement like those of a modern, normal play" (Marquerie, 196). When one views Salom's drama as a modern tragedy, his use of archetypes becomes justified.[16] Indeed, the juxtaposition of two planes of reality—Fernando's inner world and the external action—is present also in the theater of Arthur Miller, whose *Death of a Salesman* (1949) is often considered the prototype of modern tragedy. In the opening scene of the play, Fernando reveals that he is now aware of the emptiness of his own existence and the decadence of the society he is inheriting. Having come to this realization and fully aware of his own past shortcomings, he attempts reforms, summoning up a newfound strength of character and nobility of purpose. Opposed by his implacable mother and the forces she represents, and beset as always by a lack of communication with his fellow human beings, Fernando's efforts are doomed to failure. Acknowledging defeat, he commits suicide.

Fernando's failure on a political level may be attributed to those who desperately fight to maintain a dying system. On a personal level, his tragedy is that of the isolated individual. Underlying the action of the play is the lack of communication; the alternating monologues serve to reinforce this theme and must, therefore, be considered an essential structural element. In part the absence of real dialogue results from the political and social antagonisms, in part from the generation gap. The children go their separate ways, only returning home for the patriarch's birthday or deaths in the family. Carolina and Luisa will not listen when Tina tries to tell them she is in love; they will not participate in the wedding when they learn that she is marrying beneath her social status. Fernando and Fere, who might have been supportive of one another, seldom communicate directly, although in a final phone call, Fere does say that he loves his father (D, 284). It is for Fere that Fernando writes his confession: "I must write in order not to feel so alone, so that someone someday, somewhere can understand me . . . or at least feel compassion for me. Perhaps my son . . ." (D, 281). Even this hope is destroyed when Carolina burns her dead son's memoirs.

The failure of Fernando's marriage and his ensuing relationship with Susana, somewhat like the similar situation in *Lemon Peel*, have their roots both in social stratification and personal loneliness. In Fernando's evocation of her, Luisa admits that she married him for his money (D, 249). For a while she did love him, but then she was attracted to Raúl, who rejected her. For Fernando Susana represents youth and sincerity; when she betrays him with Raúl, he is at first understanding. But, when it is apparent that the reformist efforts of Raúl and Fernando cannot succeed and Susana appears ready to return to Fernando, the disillusioned man realizes that the young woman's "sincerity" was a mask for opportunism. On the allegorical level, both women symbolize that segment of Spanish society, transcending specific generations that, while attracted to the progressives, ultimately allies itself with those in power even while, like Susana, deploring what the Tusers have done to the Condominas and the Braulios.[17] On the personal level, Fernando's suicide is precipitated by the knowledge that Susana never loved him for himself; rather, she has given herself to his name and position. Luisa did love him, but it is only after his death that she realizes how he was destroyed by Carolina's pressure to make him conform.

The scene in the drama that has been singled out by several of the critics, including those who attacked the play, as being the most convincing on a human level, is one in the second act between Fernando and Braulio. Now physically alone for the first time in his life—the children are gone and the women have left Spain to avoid being embarrassed by Tina's wedding—Fernando attempts to establish a line of communication with Braulio. As Fernando observes, they have known each other all their lives: "Few have lived together so close and so far apart," (*D*, 296). At one time they fought over the same bicycle, but then Braulio learned that the bicycle was Fernando's, not his. He learned his place and has remained always in it. Fernando wonders why Braulio does not join the workers in their strike. He even invites Braulio to flee with him. But Braulio's loyalty to his place cannot be shaken. "You are like my father, unmovable, proud, hard . . ." (*D*, 299). "You are more a Tuser than I" (*D*, 300). The legacy of the Tuser dynasty is a rigid compartmentalization. Separated by social class and age, unwilling or unable to change, individuals are isolated from one another and entrapped by the material comforts they have acquired through conformity. If the defenders of the status quo prove triumphant, the only escape will continue to be death or exile.

II   Tiempo de espadas

María Luz Morales, reacting to its Barcelona premiere, correctly predicted that *The Heirs Apparent* would not please everyone because it is a polemical work.[18] *Tiempo de espadas* [Time of Swords], although not subject to the same negative criticism as the earlier drama with respect to its theatrical merits, similarly gave rise to considerable controversy. Both in Madrid, where it opened in September, 1972, and in Salom's native city, where it was staged in October of the following year, *Time of Swords* caused "an intense, shall we say, sociomoral commotion along with a great ideological confusion."[19] The controversy in fact surfaced even before the premiere; the Catalan's modernization of the Christ story was his first play to be delayed by the censor.[20]

Structurally, *Time of Swords* is a much simpler play than most of Salom's theater written in the late 1960s and early 1970s. Gone, for example, are the multiple planes of reality, fluidity of time, and doubling. Adhering to the three unities, time and action are limited to the night of the Last Supper; the single stage setting, almost devoid of furniture and props, merely suggests an open area adjoining a dining room in a supper club.[21] The meaning of the play, however, functions continuously on two levels. The story is clearly that of Christ and his twelve disciples, but time is the present. The scene is both Jerusalem, a city occupied by the Romans, and a modern city in some unspecified country where diverse political groups have formed a resistance movement in opposition to a repressive and corrupt regime. Their leader, whose forceful but enigmatic personality hovers always in the background, never appears on stage.[22]

Salom establishes the first level of interpretation by introducing biblical passages at the beginning and end of each act. Taken from the Gospel according to St. Luke, these passages include the one from which the title of the play is drawn: "And let him who has no sword sell his mantle and buy one" (Luke 22:36). The second level is established not only by modifying the names of disciples (Lebel, Santón, Karioth, Simon, Leví, Dimo, Andy, Pier, Natel, Philip, Jac, and Jano) but also by making reference to modern inventions (subways, machine guns, jeeps). The twelve men are simultaneously the apostles, who have not yet understood Christ's message, and representatives of contemporary political positions ranging from that of the conservative Leví, to the moderate democrats Jac and Jano, to the terrorist Lebel. The characters also include Max, the collaborationist maitre d'; his wife Ruth, a former terrorist companion of Lebel; and Maggi, a woman of easy virtue but fiercely loyal to Christ, who is obviously modeled after Mary Magdalene. Just as the drama's action is both now and in the past, its theme is both political and religious. For this reason, the playwright correctly sees *Time of Swords*, his favorite work to date, as being a continuation to some extent of both *The Heirs Apparent* and *The Empty Beach*.[23]

The source of controversy stemming from *Time of Swords* is twofold: the portrayal of Christ's disciples in a political rather than a religious context, and the assertion that even two thousand years after the Crucifixion, Pentecost has not yet arrived. The twelve men are divided among themselves. Simon wants to try Leví as an alleged collaborationist. Jac and Jano oppose Pier's being named as the leader's successor. Santón and Pier both suggest that Christ may not share their political goals, but in general they all continue to see their leader, even after his arrest and sentencing, only in terms of a promised revolution. It is Maggi in the concluding scene who proclaims that they do not understand and that Christ will be resurrected. Nevertheless, Pentecost, with its clarification of the meaning of Christ's life and death, will escape them: "And after forty-nine days, the Holy Spirit descended upon them, upon all of us. . . . Dear God! How long those days, those years, those twenty centuries of errors, cruelty, and incomprehension will be while waiting for your true and definitive Pentecost!"[24] The objections of Pilar Urbano are perhaps typical. She criticizes Salom for failing to underscore the spiritual mission of Christ on earth, for turning the Last Supper into a political gathering, and for ignoring the fact that twenty centuries of history have taken place since Pentecost.[25] The basic question posed to the playwright in interview after interview was that of his intended meaning. Is he really attacking Christ's disciples and/or is he denouncing contemporary society for its failure to put Christ's teachings into practice?

Salom's response in his various public statements has been uniform. His initial purpose was to write a theological play. To that end, he undertook an intensive study of the subject, including radical theology. As a result, he concluded that the real disciples were, in fact, revolutionaries seeking national liberation, albeit from varying ideological perspectives. The transition from a demythification of the past to a denunciation of the present followed naturally. "The demythification of the great myths of the history of humanity makes us pose again, from new angles, the fundamental problems of existence."[26] "Upon bringing the myth closer to us, it exploded in a profusion of surprises and interminable accusations, applicable to all times, including ours."[27] Although to use Christ for a particular political cause is a betrayal of His doctrine, "one cannot separate Christ from the temporal problems of humanity. To speak of Christ is to speak of mankind and perhaps the inverse as well."[28] Throughout his discussions of the drama, Salom has reaffirmed his own belief in Christ.

As in *The Heirs Apparent,* each of the characters may be seen as a representative figure, symbolizing a particular political attitude. Salom states that in *Time of Swords* he has presented an objective testimony to contemporary society and thus has not identified with a particular ideological view. Although in this sense the play offers no specific political solution, the playwright suggests that the solution is there: "What matters to Christ is the human being, which does not mean that Christ does not have a political position but that it is a deeper and broader one."[29]

In spite of the divergent views of the various characters and in spite of Salom's avowed effort to remain totally objective, leaving interpretation up to each spectator, certain concepts do emerge from the text as indisputable. The current regime is a repressive one that denies individual freedom. When Christ is arrested, all of his followers risk persecution, even if they, too, have committed no crimes. Leví protests that he cannot be prosecuted under Article 63 of the Internal Security Act, but Natel assures him that they all have broken this law: "Anyone who thinks, who suffers, who shows compassion for others, who rejects masters and slaves, who desires equality, everyone who is conscious of the injustice of this situation has to be an enemy" (S, 142). In the end the men are only able to avoid arrest because Ruth persuades Max to help them escape.

Even if the disciples are not sure what Christ's mission is, his message of love for humanity is in clear opposition to the practices of any repressive regime: "He speaks of justice, of liberty and of peace, although that is what all politicians in the world say and have said. . . , but is he a politician?" (S, 113). Leví asks this question: the answer, voiced in one way or another by several of the characters in the course of their anguished evening, is that he is not a politician in a narrow sense and to attempt to identify him with any particular ideology is to fail to understand him. Pier asserts that Christ's ideas do not agree with those of any of them: "Not with your action nor with his liberalism, and even less with the privileged minority. But he also does not disagree. Mankind, the human being . . . Jac and Jano, just as much as I, the invader the same as the patriots" (S, 118). Similarly, Lebel concludes, "Each of us seeks something different in our leader, and the curious thing is that we all believe we have found it, collaborationists and revolutionaries, bourgeois and workers, rich and poor. . . . Because it doesn't matter to him what we are just so long as we love" (S, 125).

Although the disciples reveal at least a superficial understanding of Christ's message, through their conduct they betray him directly or indirectly. According to Maggi, those who conspire against Christ and cause his arrest "are not their people, but ours" (S, 121), not the repressive regime, but the national liberationists. Karioth eventually confesses to Lebel that his faction had arranged the betrayal. Karioth himself had been deceived into believing the arrest would be the catalyst for open rebellion as all of the bands joined together to free their leader; in fact, the purpose was to eliminate a force his coconspirators felt detracted from their revolutionary movement. No one had risen to Christ's defense: not the disciples, not the political groups, not the totalitarian regime, not the people who only the Sunday before had thronged the streets of Jerusalem to acclaim him.

All of the disciples, not just Karioth, stand accused of the betrayal on two levels. As representatives of varying ideologies, they had attempted to use Christ for political purposes and had therefore failed to perceive his mission. Moreover, because they had remained divided among themselves, their factionalism had led to the persecution of their leader by their common enemy. Natel summarizes their political responsibility: "A while ago we tried to discover a traitor. Nothing easier: a spurt of political fanaticism of any brand, some drops of panic and a pinch of egotism. Mix well and serve without ice. You'll have your traitor within reach, anybody's reach" (S, 136). The disciples are also guilty of betrayal on a personal level, and this responsibility extends beyond them to everyone. In an impassioned monologue, Lebel turns to the audience and accuses them all of being betrayers of Christ. So that they can continue satisfying their physical and material desires—by committing adultery or fraud, by signing unjust contracts, by ignoring the problems of the poor—they would all prefer to get Christ out of the way: "We want to forget him, as if he had never existed" (S, 140–41). Karioth, in defending himself to Lebel, states that he is the other's mirror image. After Karioth's suicide, Lebel accepts the truth of that assertion; they all see themselves reflected in Karioth's action, and from their own sense of guilt they repudiate him without the love and compassion that Christ would have shown.

Lebel's confrontation with the audience is a somewhat more extensive and dramatic speech than the similar one of Fere in *The Heirs Apparent*. In both cases Salom's intention is the same. He wishes to bear witness not only to the failings of the characters within his play but also to those of contemporary society in general. Luis María Ansón, who finds this tendency in *The Empty Beach* as well as in *Time of Swords*, describes Salom's theater as one of denunciation, a theater "that tears away masks and places a mirror up to bare faces."[30] Ansón further notes that by using the "eternal language of symbols" the playwright is able to achieve his purpose. Even if some critics overlooked the symbolism of *The Heirs Apparent* at the time, a careful reading of the drama from the perspective of the present does make clear the underlying disquietude vis-à-vis political and social reality. In *The Empty Beach* the sense of anguish emanates from personal and religious preoccupations. *Time of Swords* combines the two themes, giving a more complete portrayal of Salom's concern for humanity. He suggests not only that the status quo is unacceptable but that the individual, in committing himself or herself to necessary reforms, cannot separate the political from the religious, the social from the moral. It is a time for action, but that action must be directed by Christ's message of love and justice.

Salom's mature plays, from *The Heirs Apparent* on, are at least superficially quite different from his early moralistic dramas. At the beginning of his theatrical career, the playwright limited himself to individual questions of guilt and responsibility, imposing solutions and judgments based on a narrow interpretation of Catholic doctrine. In the later works, Salom's accusing finger is pointed at everyone, including the conservative Spanish society whose values he had previously defended. Gone are the simple or narrow solutions to problems, as Salom widens his sphere of interest and becomes more compassionate and flexible in his view of right and wrong. In spite of this obvious ideological and moral evolution, the Catalan does remain consistent throughout his theater in his abiding concern for the internal conflicts of human beings and the role that religious beliefs could or should play in relieving anguish. The image of God that he conveys in *The Empty Beach* and of Christ in *Time of Swords* is that of a compassionate and loving Being, offering consolation to troubled individuals in an anxious world.

In his essay on radical theology in the theater, written before the premiere of *Time of Swords* but reflecting his research for that drama, Salom asserts that the contemporary period is undergoing a transformation as fundamental as that of the Renaissance. Whenever mankind makes a radical change in the understanding of people and their world, it "seems to lose God, because the image that man had of God was too closely tied to his own image in the world that he has just overcome" (Marquerie, 31). Although some philosophers have proclaimed that God is dead, it is not true that God has no meaning for people today. "I believe that the theological theme appeals deeply to man today and always, even in spite of himself, even if he doesn't realize it" (Marquerie, 27). Theology belongs not only to the theologians but to everyone, and especially to the theater, which should provide an analytical criticism of the individual and the society of his time. "Is it not the unrenounceable mission of the theater to interrogate, to disturb, to scrutinize, to testify?" (Marquerie, 28).

With *Time of Swords*, Salom has achieved his goal of creating a provocative theological drama. Widely acclaimed as the Catalan's most ambitious, significant, and universal work, his modernization of the Christ story, along with the debates it inspired, has been one of the major events in the Spanish theater of the 1970s. As one critic has noted, "When a play causes one of the liveliest political polemics emanating from the theater that we have known, when it is perfectly constructed and has a high theatrical quality, when the public follows it expectantly and you can hear a pin drop in the theater, when all this occurs, you have to take that play into account and face it, agreeing or disagreeing, but with respect."[31]

III *Nueve brindis por un rey*

Less successful than *Time of Swords* but equally polemical, Salom's next original play was the historical farce *Nueve brindis por un rey* [Nine Toasts for a King], a deliberately anachronistic presentation of the fifteenth-century Convention of Caspe. The playwright spent two years researching his subject and a year writing his script. The premiere, which eventually took place September 27, 1974, in Madrid, was delayed for nine months by the censor.[32]

In 1410 Martín, *el Humano*, king of Aragon, Cataluña, and Valencia, died without naming an heir; two years later, nine representatives, three from each of the affected regions, met at Caspe to elect the new king. About this historic episode there have developed two diametrically opposed schools of thought. The meeting at Caspe was either a legal convention, serving as a model for democracy, or a travesty of justice. Salom's research led him to accept the latter view, represented by the Catalan historians Domenech i Muntaner and de Ferrán Soldevila, over the more traditional opinion, as expressed by the Castilian scholar Menéndez Pidal.[33] In so choosing, Salom exposed his farce not only to difficulties with the censor but also to subsequent attacks from conservative critics and playgoers.

Throughout the ensuing controversy, the playwright repeatedly clarified that the version of history he had been taught in school, namely, that Caspe had been a peaceful and legal expression of the will of the people, was not that at all. As had happened in his previous research on Christ's disciples, Salom found a totally different reality under the surface legend. Caspe had been the culmination of a series of political and military maneuvers arising from interregional rivalries and from the Great Schism. The most legitimate claim on the throne was that of the Conde de Urgel, but Fernando de Antequera became king because his succession served the interests of Aragon and of the Avignon pope Benedict XIII. Between the death of Martín, *el Humano,* and the settlement at Caspe, an archbishop had been assassinated, thousands had died in the bloody battle of Murverdre, Spanish soil had been invaded by foreign troops, and the regional parliaments had been subjected to months of propaganda and blackmail. The nine delegates to Caspe were imposed by the parliament of Aragon, and in fact the people were not involved in the selection of their supposed representatives.[34] Salom determined to reveal the truths he had found behind the legend: "The myth of history is one of the great repressive weapons that has been used for centuries to humiliate the younger generations, who can only kneel down before such weighty proof of irrefutable grandeur and glory."[35] Not excluded from the demythification process is the Spanish saint Vicente Ferrer, who is characterized by Salom as a fascist philosopher quite capable of human error.[36]

Like *Time for Swords*, the action in *Nine Toasts for a King* functions simultaneously on two temporal levels. The farce is intended not only to debunk the myth of Caspe as a model of democracy but also to satirize the contemporary political situation. Carried to its logical parallel, the play warns that after Franco the Spanish government may continue to be controlled by the vested interests of an antidemocratic minority. Certainly Juan Carlos, who was to become king, had not been chosen by the people to succeed the dictator. Franco was not to die until a year after Salom's play was staged; the subject of what political changes would take place after his death was still taboo. According to Salom, the contemporary ramifications of his criticism evoked even greater hostility and indignation than his satire of Caspe. He received letters and phone calls protesting that his work should have been definitively prohibited by the censor.[37]

Salom's use of Spanish history to make an oblique commentary on his own time is, of course, not unique in contemporary theater.

Beginning with Buero Vallejo's *Un soñador para un pueblo* [A Dreamer for a People, 1958], there has been a vogue of historical plays of allegorical intent, ranging from serious drama to farce. The trend has continued into the 1970s. The same year that *Nine Toasts for a King* was staged also saw the premieres of Ana Diosdado's *Los comuneros* [The Rebels] and Antonio Gala's *Las cítaras colgadas de los árboles* [Zithers Hanging from the Trees]. Although Diosdado's presentation of the sixteenth-century popular uprising against Carlos I is serious in tone, Salom's farce is somewhat related to it in its fluidity of movement in time and space and in the use of doubling so that an individual character assuming various roles may participate in widely separated scenes. While the history plays in Franco Spain were at least in part a reaction to censorship, they also belong to a more universal current. In particular, critics justifiably identified a certain influence of Bertolt Brecht (1898–1956) on *Nine Toasts for a King*, although they might also have cited Max Frisch's *The Chinese Wall*, a historical farce that Salom had adapted for a 1971 production in Madrid. The Swiss play explores humanity's chance of avoiding total destruction by the atom bomb, but the action takes place in China during the completion of the Great Wall.

In portraying the events leading up to the Convention of Caspe, Salom chose to eliminate from his cast the principal historical figures: Martín, *el Humano*, the Conde de Urgel, Fernando de Antequera, and Benedict XIII. Instead, his protagonist is Guillermo de Vallseca, a Catalan delegate to Caspe who cast the lone vote for Urgel. Vallseca is a jurist and an expert on civil law; he is a man of integrity with an unswerving dedication to justice. Although Juan Emilio Aragonés has somewhat exaggerated the dichotomy between the favorable portrayal of Vallseca and the satirical treatment of the other delegates when he suggests that *Nine Toasts for a King* resembles a Western with one good guy standing up to a band of bad guys,[38] it is true that Vallseca generally escapes the play's dominantly farcical tone. While most of the characters at one time or another are depicted as caricatures rather than real people, Vallseca remains an anguished human being. At least superficially, Salom's technique is not unlike that of Ramón del Valle-Inclán's *Luces de bohemia* [Bohemian Lights, 1924] in which the protagonist, Max Estrella, is not submitted to the same deliberate process of deformation as are most of the other characters.

The conflict confronting Vallseca in various forms is that between justice and political expediency. The Catalan jurist is forced into making difficult and unpopular decisions even before the king's death. In an early scene from the first act, he is asked by Fray Francisco de Aranda to validate a declaration, obtained from the king on his deathbed by several members of parliament, that his throne go to the most deserving heir. Believing the declaration to be illegal, Vallseca refuses to comply: "Fray Francisco de Aranda, neither you, nor the king, nor the pope, nor God himself can ask me, without gravely offending me, that I approve with my signature such an arbitrary act!" (B, 16). It is with this same intransigence that Vallseca will maintain that Urgel is the rightful heir. In that Martín dies without recognizing an illegitimate son and hence his grandson, Federico, el Bastardo, the throne must pass to the heir of one of his brothers. But two of the king's brothers had daughters, and Vallseca affirms that the Salic law, prohibiting succession through females, must be observed because Martín himself had become king on precisely that legal principle. By this reasoning, both Luis de Anjou and Fernando de Antequera are eliminated from consideration.

To Vallseca's insistence on a strict interpretation of the law is added his growing commitment to democracy. His concern for the people is deepened in part by the comforting presence of Lucía, a slave who has been sent to Vallseca by a priest to help care for him during an attack of gout. He seeks her opinions only to learn that she has none. "I don't think, my lord. It's prohibited by the Code. Twenty lashes for the servant who has an idea of her own. Article 31" (B, 12). If the people were allowed to think, she would elect the king who would give her freedom (B, 22). Later Vallseca describes to several of the delegates a procedure by which all the men in the kingdom would write their choices on pieces of paper, and the candidate with the largest number of votes would be declared the winner. The others scoff at the concepts, particularly the idea of counting the votes to learn the results. "God knows, and that's enough," explains the archbishop of Tarragona (B, 29). In the growing ideological struggle between Vallseca and the others, the Catalan jurist protests, as did Fernando in The Heirs Apparent, that the name of God is being used by the antidemocratic forces to circumvent justice and the law. He tells Vicente Ferrer, "With all respect, neither you nor any of us can domesticate God like a household pet" (B, 73). Significantly, the priest who lent Lucía to Vallseca refuses to sell her when he learns that the jurist's intention is to free her. In the end, when Vallseca knows that his adherence to truth at Caspe will cost him dearly, he orders his son Fabián and Lucía to flee to Navarre, where slavery has been abolished and she will find liberty.

Vallseca is clearly intended to be a strong voice for Salom's own liberal political views, but his message is overshadowed by the theatrical elements of the play. The structure is episodic, with scene changes facilitated by a large revolving platform that occupies most of the stage. Various segments are introduced by a series of satirical songs, and in other ways as well the work is treated as a spectacle. The impending Convention at Caspe is announced by Fabián, in the role of news vendor, shouting out the headlines. The partisans of the various pretenders to the throne are presented as delegates at an American political convention, waving banners and yelling slogans. A number of the scenes are built on well-established farcical devices. The mothers of Urgel and Anjou, for example, have comic fights, complete with name-calling. Anjou's mother at one point is in a bathtub filled with soap suds. Angered by the political stance of one of the men, she jumps from the tub—clad in an old-fashioned bathing suit—and chases him with a hairbrush. Vallseca, the archbishop of Tarragona, and Fray Francisco de Aranda have one of their most profound discussions while playing golf.[39] Deliberate anachronisms of this type abound, serving both for comic effect and to convey a contemporary meaning to the fifteenth-century events.

Nine Toasts for a King is highly theatrical and overtly theatricalist. Characters self-consciously act out their historical roles, letting each other and the audience know what the future holds in store. When the archbishop of Zaragoza is about to be murdered by one of Urgel's supporters, he is not sure for what cause he is dying, but he does remind his assassin that he is to be killed with a sword, not a dagger. At the Convention of Caspe itself, the bishop of Huesca reads to the others from the historical account of their meeting. In the final scene of the play, the nine representatives to Caspe hold champagne glasses as if making a toast to the new king. Instead, each identifies himself and recounts his life and accomplishments after the Convention. Only Vallseca has nothing to tell, for the history books never mention him again; in spirit if not in body, he died at Caspe.

As in the plays of poetic fantasy, Salom makes uses of doubling to emphasize the nonrepresentational aspect of his play. Near the beginning of the farce, Vallseca and Lucía put on masks to act out the roles of the aging king and his virgin queen. When Urgel's mother visits Vallseca to tell him of her unsuccessful efforts at having the king recognize her son as his heir, she casts the jurist into the king's role and almost chokes him to death. In addition to these brief scenes, an extensive use of doubling is found throughout the farce in the character of Fabián, whose appearance in a dozen guises serves as a unifying thread for the many episodes. With his songs and announcements, he performs an important narrative function. His principal role is that of Vallseca's son and companion, but in his many subroles he is included among the supporters for each of the pretenders to the throne. At the end of the play, Vallseca makes it clear that Fabián's doubling bears a message. "Have you never asked yourself what role we've given you in this farce? Servant to obey our orders, secretary to take dictation, soldier to die, messenger without the right to change the message, policeman to defend our privileges. A mere extra for an all-powerful generation" (B, 80). Fabián is intended to represent the younger generation that has been manipulated by its elders in the pursuit of political causes. On a note of hope, Vallseca tells his son that now his own play and his own role are beginning; perhaps, but only perhaps, he can avoid the pitfalls of the past.

From the standpoint of both critical reaction and popular appeal, *Nine Toasts for a King* has been the least successful of Salom's plays of political and social commentary. Some of the negative response may be attributed to ideological opposition, but other reservations about the work are more valid. Highly complex in its story and staging, *Nine Toasts for a King* is different in many ways from any of Salom's previous ventures. It is his first effort at blending a kind of theatrical spectacle—earlier found to a limited extent in his plays of light entertainment—with a level of serious social criticism. For some critics at least, the direction of Alberto González Vergel was not adequate to the challenge while for others the best aspect of the farce was its staging.[40] Unquestionably, the most obvious difficulty with the text is the historical basis itself. The events between the death of Martín, *el Humano*, and the meeting at Caspe are complicated and relatively unfamiliar even to Spanish audiences.[41] At times the explanation of what is happening, some of it rather technical, slows the action of the play but still leaves the reader, let alone the spectator, somewhat bewildered. Vallseca's illustrated lecture with an illuminated genealogical chart is essential to understanding the plot but also highlights its basic shortcoming. Of equal importance is the question of tone. Salom is not fully successful in integrating the farcical elements with his serious commentary. Although several critics were reminded of Valle-Inclán's *esperpento*, the comparison is not totally justified. Valle's caricatures are shown as grotesque figures, while Salom's tend to be merely ridiculous. It is probably for that reason that the satire is not so effective as it might be and that the work does not form a harmonious whole.

IV   La piel del limón

No less polemical than *Nine Toasts for a King* but a much more effective work, *La piel del limón* [Lemon Peel] was also directed by González Vergel. It opened in Madrid in September, 1976, and enjoyed a run of more than five hundred performances. Widely recognized as an impassioned plea for divorce reform in Spain, it not only culminates the series of plays of political and social commentary but also presents the playwright's most sophisticated development to date of various techniques associated with other currents in his theater: externalization of psychological conflicts, fluidity of time, and doubling. In structure, it is clearly a return from the kind of Brechtian spectacle that Salom attempted in his historical farce to a more subjective drama.[42] Unlike the previous plays discussed in this chapter, the cast is small—only five actors—and the characters in general are portrayed as individual human beings rather than symbolic figures. Nevertheless, *Lemon Peel* continues in the vein of *The Heirs Apparent* as a denunciation of the rigidity and hypocrisy that Salom finds in certain sectors of contemporary Spanish society.

The protagonist of the drama is Juan, a successful businessman who would like to leave his wife Rosa in order to live with Bárbara, the woman he loves. Although he considers his marriage long since dead—like a lemon "it can be rotten on the inside but the peel always remains shiny and whole" (*L*, 21)—he is torn between his love for Bárbara and his love for his teenage daughter Alejandra. As the author explains in his self-criticism, it is precisely to give visual form to Juan's inner struggle that he decided to have the same actress play both roles (*L*, 8). Bárbara, however, never intervenes in the real action of the drama. On the level of reality, Juan is home with his family. Bárbara appears on the retrospective level of Juan's thoughts as he remembers her and relives their love story. The two planes— the present reality and the remembered past—exist simultaneously; the characters move from one plane to another without interruption.

The real action in the first act takes place during Alejandra's thirteenth birthday party. The family's two guests are Narciso, Rosa's cousin and Juan's business associate, and Ernestina, Rosa's best friend who has also been Juan's secret lover. Even within this plane of reality there are two levels: the superficial one of happiness, friendship, and family affection and the underlying one in which the inner conflicts are slowly revealed, leading up to Juan's announcement at the end of the act that he is leaving Rosa. On the retrospective plane Juan relives episodes in his affair with Bárbara. The sequence of events in the past is chronological, ending with the current emotional crisis that has precipitated his decision to separate from his wife.

The second act begins with a birthday party almost identical to the first one. Only gradually do we learn that three years have passed and that the external action of the play will now be inverted. Juan— defeated by an intransigent society that prohibits divorce, by the machinations of his business associate who has a greater concern for lost profits than for lost love, and by his own rigid upbringing that burdens him with guilt—has agreed to return to Rosa and their hollow marriage. On the retrospective plane, the action presents first the life of Juan and Bárbara together and then, when their chance for happiness has been destroyed, selected moments from previous scenes. All that remains for Juan are memories; Bárbara has disappeared. Without Juan's knowledge, Narciso convinced Bárbara that their situation was impossible and that Juan could not be happy either leaving his company to start over elsewhere or watching his business suffer because of his clients' indignation at his open violation of society's moral code. Still in love with Juan, but not wanting him to suffer because of her, Bárbara has apparently committed suicide.

The juxtaposition of Juan's two worlds serves a dual function. It visualizes his internal conflict, thus contributing to the psychological development of his character, and it creates a high level of dramatic irony. In the first act, Juan's fantasy makes clear the hypocrisy involved in the festive atmosphere and the bonds of affection. In the second act, the inevitability of his failure makes more poignant his search for happiness.

In *Lemon Peel*, Salom combines various of the approaches to doubling introduced in earlier plays. The instantaneous transitions from one role to another, briefly used in *The Trunk of Disguises* and *Nine Toasts for a King*, are perfected here. The freezing of characters on one level of reality while the action moves to the other, previously utilized in the second act of *Saturday Night Date*, is given extensive treatment in the later drama. In the Madrid production of *Lemon Peel*, the actors in the present stayed on stage, immobile, during Juan's memories. Appropriate changes in lighting facilitated the transition. Narciso, as well as Juan, moves continually between present and past, between Juan's marriage and his love affair. The actress playing the dual roles of Alejandra and Bárbara is called upon to shift constantly from one character to the other and portray convincingly both the teenage girl and the thirty-year-old woman.

The psychological implications possible in the doubling technique, hinted at in *Parcheesi Party,* are fully exploited in *Lemon Peel.* The inner conflict represented by Alejandra-Bárbara is verbalized by Juan in the second act during a scene that is in effect a flashback-within-a-flashback. On the subjective plane of Juan's thoughts, he recalls a conversation with Bárbara in which he tells her of Alejandra's visit to his office. That second moment from the past is presented in counterpoint with the Bárbara–Juan dialogue, thus placing the actress in the position of portraying almost simultaneously Alejandra in the present (age sixteen), Alejandra in the past (age thirteen), and Bárbara. Juan complains to Bárbara that sending Alejandra to see him was a trap: "Do you know what they're trying to do? Confront the two of you, turn you into rivals, put me in the spot of choosing between my daughter and you" (*L,* 52). Through the doubling, Salom has indeed brought the two characters together, visualizing Juan's anguish. He reinforces the merging of the two in Juan's mind by having the characters speak of one another in almost identical words. When Juan first leaves his family, Bárbara asks him, "Do you think about them?" and he replies, "Sometimes. I can't help it" (*L,* 44). The dialogue is repeated upon his return home when Alejandra asks, "Do you think about her?" and Juan once again responds, "Sometimes. I can't help it" (*L,* 66).[43]

Salom does not limit either the juxtaposition of temporal planes or the use of doubling to Juan's current conflicts. Within his memories, Juan reverts to his adolescent years. Suddenly the mature actor doubles in the role of the boy, while the actresses become his mother and the young Rosa and Narciso is transformed into the father superior of young Juan's Catholic school. The scene is a comic one, reminiscent of a moment in Jean Anouilh's *Les Poissons rouges* [The Red Fish] in which the middle-aged actor similarly assumes the role of the child. The French play, which bears some coincidental resemblance to Salom's drama both structurally and thematically, was staged in Madrid in 1973 and again in 1974.

The scene from Juan's youth functions as comic relief, but it also establishes a theme of social criticism that goes beyond the mere absence of a divorce law. Juan sees himself as the victim of his education. During the first party, Ernestina asks him what he really desires. He responds that he would like to begin again and be a different person: "They needed twenty years of sermons and discipline to make me what I am, to form my mentality, my way of thinking. And when they finally succeeded, I find that I am carrying a ridiculous dead weight on my shoulders that has nothing to do with real life . . ." (L, 30–31). In his comic role as father superior, Narciso serves as the vehicle for Salom's satire of that education. "If you want to live, renounce life," he advises. "How to conquer the dangerous temptations of the world? . . . with an absolute submission, humility, meekness, and blind obedience to our mother church. Like a cane that lets itself be taken here and there and is a support but with no other desire than unconditional service" (L, 32). In essence Juan, like Fernando in *The Heirs Apparent,* is a protagonist-victim from the bridge generation. In his world of fantasy, Juan rebels against the father superior, protesting that his youth, his life, and his freedom have been sacrificed to meaningless words. Those of his generation are "empty and irreproachable" (L, 34). Later he laments that he does not know how to face his life or his truth. "It is so difficult to live in the 70s when you were educated in the 50s" (L, 40).

Juan identifies with his generation and places himself in the larger social context, but he is not intended to be a symbolic figure. The only character who does not emerge as a real human being is Narciso. Incarnating all the worst aspects of hypocrisy and materialism, Narciso tends to be a caricature who speaks in clichés. On occasion he interrupts the action to address the audience directly or to double in some other role. In this way he serves as the comic and satiric counterbalance to the other characters. His multifaceted role not only does not destroy the unity of the principal action but in fact prevents their story from deteriorating into melodrama.

Although *Lemon Peel* presents the problem of divorce from the perspective of Juan, it does not fail to show with compassion the situation of the female characters. Rosa is inflexible in her attitudes, but she, too, is a victim. She knows that her husband has ceased to love her and that he is unfaithful, but she is impelled to fight to maintain the outer shell of an empty marriage. For her, as a Catholic, divorce would not exist even if the law recognized it. Her anguish is compounded by emotional instability and poor health. Years ago they lost a child; she and Juan continue to blame each other for the little girl's death. Rosa cannot overcome her sense of guilt; her illness is undoubtedly psychosomatic but is nonetheless real. She is as nervous as a new bride when Juan is about to return home, but she knows that their reconciliation is only a sham.

The Rosa–Juan–Bárbara triangle is somewhat analagous to the Luisa–Fernando–Susana one of *The Heirs Apparent.* In both cases,

upper-middle-class businessmen who have long since discovered that
their marriages are devoid of real affection turn to younger women,
first from physical desire and then from genuine love. Although Luisa
is temporarily attracted to another man, both wives abide by a rigid
moral code and represent a society implacably protecting the status
quo. Bárbara and Susana, on the other hand, are women of a lower
social class who work for their living, have little tolerance for the
superficialities of the wealthy, and feel no guilt about the series of
love affairs they have experienced. For Juan–Fernando, they represent authenticity and freedom. The social classes are the reverse of
those in *The Night of the Hundred Birds*, but again the married man
is seeking an illusive happiness in the form of a younger woman who
seems less bound by the limits of her daily existence than he is. In the
two earlier plays, Salom disillusions his protagonists with respect to
the women they love; neither Lilián nor Susana are what Adrián and
Fernando believe them to be. In *Lemon Peel*, the playwright creates
a strong feminist character who remains true to herself and to her love
for Juan.

The most complex and interesting of the female characters in the
drama, Bárbara is the spokesperson for a philosophy of life that is
antithetical to the conservative moralistic attitude found in Salom's
earlier plays. Her life, from childhood on, has been a difficult and
even sordid one. Her marriage, like Juan's, is long since dead, and
she has no real feeling for the man with whom she is living when her
affair with Juan begins. Nevertheless, she is still an idealist who
believes that happiness is possible, not in renunciation but in giving
oneself fully to life and love. She insists upon equality in her relationship with Juan—rebuking him for applying a double standard of
sexual morality and for his outbursts of jealousy about her past—but
responds to their love with a contagious and youthful enthusiasm.
She feels that Juan has never really lived. He has been a slave to his
work and his money; he has never freely chosen anything, including
his wife. Their love is his first authentic self-expression. Juan agrees,
but in the end he is not strong enough to break with his past. Even
before Narciso persuades her to leave Juan, Bárbara realizes that he
cannot abandon everything to go off with her and start anew. "My
case is different," she tells him. "I have always been an outsider."
Juan can neither give up his wealth and social standing nor rid himself
of guilt. "You feel as if you had commited a crime, and you only hope
that they will forgive you. . . . You aren't guilty. I'd give anything to
make you understand that. All we want is to live our love" (*L*, 57).

That love is doomed to failure in a country that prohibits divorce and insists that the sanctity of marriage be honored, if only in appearance. Repeating the criticism of a decadent society introduced in *The Heirs Apparent*, Bárbara proclaims that she and Juan are "prisoners in a world of madmen . . . that is approaching its end" (*L*, 58).

In his obvious plea for divorce reform, Salom tends to sermonize, sometimes in the speeches of Bárbara, sometimes in those of Juan.[44] Although the attacks on what they consider to be antiquated laws are not inconsistent with the emotional state of the two characters, the result is rather didactic. Somewhat more subtle and hence more effective is the revelation of the reality behind the marriages that the dominantly Catholic society wants to preserve. Juan's crime is not in falling in love with another woman but in trying to live that love openly and authentically. Narciso, who pontificates for the family— "The family is the foundation of society and civilization. If such a sacred bond were destroyed, everything would topple: banks, industries, finance, and commerce" (*L*, 15)—nevertheless advises Juan how he can manage an affair with Bárbara and maintain his respectability: "Give her some money and take her with you, discreetly, on your business trips" (*L*, 16). Narciso's lesson on adultery is one that Ernestina has learned well. Her marriage, too, is devoid of love, but she can at least achieve physical pleasure if she carefully separates her public and private lives. She sees no hypocrisy in her friendship with Rosa and does not object to Juan's infidelity provided that he continues to be her lover: "As long as our affair remains in its compartment, nothing else matters to me" (*L*, 24). A victim of her generation like Rosa and Juan, Ernestina has found in her friend's husband a safe way of satisfying her human needs without sacrificing appearance.

Salom posits divorce reform as at least a partial solution to the pervasive unhappiness and moral hypocrisy that he identifies in Spanish society, but even within the context of his drama it is clear that a mere revision in the law cannot solve all of the human problems caused by the disintegration of the family. Bárbara defends Alejandra when Juan relates his daughter's emotional rejection of him. "She isn't to blame; she didn't invent the system. . . . It is your world, your country, your church that closed the door to any reasonable solution, not your daughter" (*L*, 54). While Alejandra's trauma, like that of her mother, is compounded by the social situation and their religious upbringing, the adolescent's anguish transcends those limitations. At thirteen she loves her father deeply and responds emotionally when he abandons her and her mother to be with another woman. She is on the verge of womanhood herself, but in some ways she is still a child. She considers Bárbara a rival; her jealousy is quite realistic in psychological terms. At sixteen she displays a new maturity and hence a better understanding of her father. In his portrayal of Alejandra, Salom has captured with great sensitivity the reaction of a young girl to the matrimonial difficulties of her parents.

Less verisimilar is Bárbara's suicide, which is out of keeping with her spirit of independence, her strength of character, and her proven ability to adjust to adverse circumstances.[45] The scene leading up to her disappearance is, in fact, one that breaks the structural unity of the drama. At all other times, the action on the retrospective plane reflects the thoughts and memories of Juan. In this one instance, Narciso's visit to Bárbara is one of which Juan is unaware. Narciso's indication to Rosa in the present that Bárbara may have killed herself—a conversation that Juan also does not hear—is, however, only conjecture. Thus there remains in the characterization of Bárbara, as with Juana in *The Night of a Hundred Birds*, a certain ambiguity. If we accept Juana's death and Bárbara's disappearance as suicides, the two women, along with Trini in *The House of the "Chivas,"* respond in the same way to the basic situation in spite of their widely divergent personalities. Once they have learned the meaning of real love, they cannot continue living without it. In part Fernando's suicide in *The Heirs Apparent* is similarly a response to this disillusionment over Susana's insincerity.

In *The Heirs Apparent* and *Lemon Peel* Salom does not limit himself to the individual moral dilemmas found in most of his earlier plays. His criticism is leveled at society. The defeat of Fernando, Juan, and Bárbara may be attributed as much to the world in which they are forced to live as to themselves. *Lemon Peel* is not only one of Salom's most interesting dramas for its structural innovations and psychological development of character, but also for its impassioned plea for greater individual freedom.

CHAPTER 8

Recent Directions

IN THE several years following the successful production of *Lemon Peel*, Salom has continued his constant experimentation with various theatrical forms while expanding upon certain themes and tendencies introduced in his mature theater of the 1970s. *Intimate Stories of Paradise*, which opened in Madrid in October, 1978, is a farce that debunks the myth of Adam and Eve. *The Crusades*, a rock musical that had not yet been staged at the time of this writing, is a deliberately anachronistic presentation of thirteenth-century history. *El corto vuelo del gallo* [The Rooster's Short Flight], a polemical drama dealing with the life of Franco's father, had its premiere in Madrid in September, 1980. In spite of obvious differences in tone and structure among the three plays, they all remain within the current of Salom's theater of social and political commentary. Like *Time of Swords* and *Nine Toasts for a King*, *Intimate Stories of Paradise* and *The Crusades* are intended not only to reveal certain truths behind the historical or biblical legends but also to present a commentary on contemporary society. *The Rooster's Short Flight* has an overt purpose of opening discussion on Franco's family and thereby explain the origins of the official morality that dominated Spain for forty years. Both *Intimate Stories of Paradise* and *The Rooster's Short Flight* are directly related to *Lemon Peel* in their opposition to the traditional concept of marriage. The biblical farce also develops more fully the feminist ideology introduced in *Lemon Peel*, while *The Rooster's Short Flight* continues and elaborates the innovative staging techniques of the earlier drama.

I   Historias íntimas del paraíso

Starting with his oblique criticism of the decline of Franco Spain in *The Heirs Apparent*, Salom has not hesitated to deal with themes that are both timely and controversial. In *Lemon Peel* he not only became

124

an outspoken supporter of divorce reform but, through the character of Bárbara, gave expression to at least some tenets of the women's liberation movement. With *Intimate Stories of Paradise* he juxtaposes two diametrically opposed images of women: the traditional submissive housewife and the feminist intellectual who vocally asserts her right to full equality. Salom is reluctant to call his farce feminist, largely because he believes that it is difficult for a man to capture completely the woman's perspective: "We men have a kind of Tarzanism that is often unconscious because ours is a culture acquired across the centuries."[1] His decision to write a comedy rather than a drama about a subject he takes very seriously himself was dictated by his feeling that a male author should not attempt to speak for the feminist cause.[2] His stand in favor of women's equality is, however, unequivocal. He publicly agreed with the feminists that the new Spanish constitution, under discussion in the fall of 1978 at the time of the Madrid production of *Intimate Stories of Paradise,* is a *machista* document, among other reasons because it favors male succession to the throne.[3] Within the context of his farce, his preference for the viewpoint of his liberated female character over that of the traditional woman or of his stereotypical male chauvinist is readily apparent.

Salom prepared for his farce by immersing himself in feminist writings from various countries, particularly the United States, and by continuing his research of biblical history and legend. Turning, as many feminists have, to the myth of Adam and Eve, he began to analyze the discrepancies between the versions of creation in the first and second chapters of Genesis. Additionally, he explored medieval Hebrew legends that described Lilith, Eve's predecessor.

In the first chapter of Genesis, the Bible recounts a simultaneous creation of man and woman, implying an equality of the sexes: "So God created man in his own image, in the image of God created he him; male and female created he them." The account in the second chapter presents a sequential creation and introduces the story of woman being made from man's rib: "And the Lord God caused a deep sleep to fall upon Adam, and he slept: and he took one of his ribs, and closed up the flesh instead thereof; and the rib, which the Lord God had taken from man, made he a woman, and brought her unto the man." According to Theodor Reik, "if in one version God created man, male and female, and in the other woman was made from Adam's rib, our most distant ancestor must have been a widower or a divorced man when the Lord brought Eve to him."[4] With similar logic, Hebrew legends speak of Lilith, Adam's first wife who left him because he denied her equality. In a particular twelfth-century myth, the catalyst for Lilith's departure is a dispute over Adam's insistence upon assuming the superior position during their lovemaking. Lilith objects on the grounds that if they are equal, she should not be beneath him. When Adam attempts to force her, Lilith, in a rage, calls upon the name of God, rises in the air, and abandons him.[5]

Salom takes the story of Lilith as the basis for his plot and then creates his farce by blending a fanciful biblical setting with elements from the contemporary world. His intention, like that of classic comedy and farce, is to make his audience laugh at human foibles, especially their own, and by so doing teach them to mend their ways.[6] Unlike *Nine Toasts for a King, Intimate Stories of Paradise* is not satirical in tone and is a return to a much simpler staging and structure. The cast is limited to four characters—Adán, Lilí, Eva, and the Angel—and there is a single setting—a primitive corner of paradise, with a desk and an apple tree. Time is linear and there is only one plane of reality.

In the first act, God has just completed the creation. Adán and Lilí very quickly discover love and sex, have their first fight and first reconciliation, and, in spite of their physical compatibility, develop matrimonial difficulties. The Angel's attempts to have Adán realize that he is in the wrong meet with failure. Lilí, disturbed that Adán wishes her to be subservient to him, divorces him. In the second act, Adán persuades the Angel to make him a second wife, one who will not expect to be his equal. Adán himself suggests using his rib. Eva is all that Adán ordered, but he finds her unbearably dull and still loves Lilí. Thus adultery is invented. Eva is suspicious and jealous, but Lilí, who sometimes comes to sit in the apple tree, becomes her friend. When Lilí decides to leave paradise, Adán deliberately eats an apple so that he may be exiled with her. Eva follows suit. The Angel, who has already confided in Eva that he could not remove Adán's rib and in fact she was made from clay just like Adán and Lilí, intends to write an accurate report of what happened, but Adán insists that he will author the history himself, with a few modifications. It is Adán who creates the story of the talking serpent and of Eva's role in the loss of paradise.

Although *Intimate Stories of Paradise* is flawed, even more than *Lemon Peel*, by occasional scenes that verge on sermonizing, in general Salom succeeds in maintaining the rhythm and tone of farce. He exploits to the fullest the comic potential in a modernization of the biblical story by introducing humor based on anachronism and incongruity. Similarly, he takes advantage of the Angel's purity and Adán and Eva's initial innocence by introducing moments of risqué humor. Particularly Adán and Eva, but to a large extent the Angel and Lilí as well, are caricatures and hence fall within the tradition of farce. So do certain stock comic devices and situations, most notably the series of quarrels and husband-wife conflicts.

The action both begins and ends with the Angel. Dressed like a contemporary hotel manager and characterized as a well-intentioned but somewhat inept functionary always worried about bureaucratic evaluations of his performance in his new position, the Angel is a felicitous invention. His presence keeps the farce from degenerating into a mere ideological confrontation or domestic comedy. In an opening scene, similar in its theatricalist technique to that of *The Empty Beach*, the Angel is saying goodby to God, who is just departing in a helicopter. "It's a masterpiece," he calls out. "Have a nice weekend, Lord. You deserve a good rest."[7] The tone of the play is quickly established by the element of fantasy involved in evoking the imaginary helicopter, by the incongruity of the Angel's colloquial speech, by the playful approach to the biblical story, and by the Angel's subsequent worries and complaints. "Who's going to make everything work? Who's going to keep it in order? If something breaks down, who's going to repair it? While He's up there resting so divinely, I'm here putting up with everything" (*P*, I, 5). In spite of his surface grumbling, which continues throughout the play, it is clear that the Angel develops a real affection and compassion for his human charges, the problems they cause him notwithstanding. In the final scene, as he remains alone and disconsolate in paradise, he telephones his superiors to volunteer for the new corps of guardian angels.

The three humans are all more predictable in their characterizations than the Angel, although Salom provides a variety of surprises, particularly through his use of anachronism. Adán and Lilí wear contemporary unisex clothing—faded blue jeans and T-shirts—while Eva appears in a denim skirt replete with feminine ruffles. God left behind in paradise a number of useful books, including texts on sex education, sexual justice, and the rights of women. Lilí, whose understanding of the world around her from the moment of creation on is truly phenomonal and stands in comic contrast to the bewilderment of both Adán and the Angel, quickly sets about reading. Adán, whose male chauvinism emerges almost as soon as he becomes aware of Lilí's intelligence and talent, destroys God's books, saying he will write his own. Salom's most effective touch, however, lies not so much in the new and original but in the clever incorporation of a complete collection of clichés, canards, and trite situations dealing with sex roles and matrimonial relations. Lilí's feminist rhetoric may escape unscathed, but virtually all that Adán and Eva say or do is subject to laughter.

The playwright's purpose is abundantly clear. He wishes to debunk not only the myth of Adam and Eve but also those stereotyped notions about proper male and female roles that result in unhappy marriages. If man is not willing to accept woman as his equal, if he wants her to be "sweet, submissive, self-sacrificing, always home . . . one child after another . . . not very bright . . ." (P, I, 53), then he should not complain if she turns out to be "silly, boring, bourgeoise" (P, II, 34). It is precisely because he has insisted that his wife and mother of his children be subservient and inferior that he feels impelled to seek the companionship of a mistress. "Almost all marriages are kept intact thanks to the sacrifice of two unfortunate women," Lilí explains to Eva (P, II, 30). It is through Lilí that Salom presents his message and his plea for equality between the sexes: "This invention of men and women can function marvelously, you know; but it is so perfect and so balanced that if one of the two tugs too hard, it can be ruined in a minute" (P, I, 31).

In his self-criticism of the comedy, Salom expressed the hope that his audience would enjoy *Intimate Stories of Paradise* as much as he had enjoyed writing it. His hope was not fully realized. The reaction of at least some playgoers and critics was hostile. The playwright feels they reacted negatively to his colloquial and facetious treatment of a sacred myth, which offended them on religious grounds, and to his caricature of Eve, which traditional Spanish women took as a personal affront.[8] As Angel Cuevas observed in an interview with Salom, the feminist viewpoint is still considered a daring one in Spain: "It nevertheless requires a lot of courage to confront a topic like that on the stage particularly among us, the Celtiberians, so proud of our *machismo*."[9] Undaunted by the possibility of further controversy, the playwright responded that *machismo* reveals an inferiority complex. The farce was scheduled for a provincial tour, starting in

Zaragoza in December, 1978, and plans were underway in the spring of 1979 for a Latin American premiere in Buenos Aires.[10] While *Intimate Stories of Paradise* has some weak points, notably in the scenes that are too overtly didactic, it is basically an entertaining and clever comedy that deserved a better reception than it was given in Madrid.

II   Las cruzadas

If *Intimate Stories of Paradise* was more likely to be appreciated by foreign audiences, *Las cruzadas* [The Crusades] might not be staged in Salom's native country at all for economic reasons. "Its premiere will surely take place outside Spain because it is difficult to produce a musical comedy here without government help."[11] The musical score, composed by Juan Carlos Calderón, was not complete until the spring of 1979, but Salom's work on the project dates back several years. In 1974 he had already announced his intention of using the historical background of the Crusades in order to make a commentary on contemporary counterculture.[12] The most radical of his plays to date, *The Crusades* presents the struggle of the youth movement against the older generation, "against the system, against institutions, against a society whose foundation does not satisfy them."[13] Given its satirical tone and its episodic structure, the rock musical bears a closer relationship to *Nine Toasts for a King* than to any of Salom's other previous works.

The setting for *The Crusades* is France; the year is 1212. The protagonist is Esteban, a young shepherd who has received a mysterious letter instructing him to lead a crusade to Jerusalem. The king's advisers find Esteban dangerous and want him burned. The king protects him, however, and Esteban soon attracts a following of young people with his message of hope and peace. They will go to the promised land as a youth crusade, "without leaders, without bloodshed, without hatred, without pillaging."[14] Esteban continues on to Marseilles, gaining both disciples and enemies along the way. He is now convinced that Christ himself sent him the letter and that when he reaches the sea, the waters will miraculously part for him. The arrival at the port is followed by weeks of disillusionment when no miracle occurs. Then two merchants provide the crusaders with ships. Many of the young people set sail without Esteban, not knowing that they are being sent to exile and death by those who fear their idealism.

In the final scenes of the play, it is 1230. One of the crusaders, René, has succeeded in returning to Marseilles. The traces of the youth movement have all but disappeared. Esteban and a few others who have not sold their souls to militarism and the consumer society remain outcasts, living from charity and from selling crosses to tourists. When René refuses a hero's welcome and attempts to stir the former crusaders from their lethargy, the establishment threatens to retaliate. Rather than hide, Esteban, René, and the others decide to attack. They set fire to the brothels, the jails, the bishop's palace, and the captain's castle. At last Esteban believes he understands the letter he received years ago. Jerusalem is not a city: "Jerusalem is all of us." The sea is the sea of fire that is destroying the shackles of the past. Hope and peace may be found if all of the innocent and the pure of heart unite.

Like *Time of Swords, The Crusades* develops in some depth the relationships among several members of the band of followers and their varying reasons for joining the movement. Esteban's idealism and faith are neither shared nor understood by everyone. Rosa, a prostitute, is attracted to Esteban not by ideology but by desire. Lucía, the niece of the king's own priest, is less pragmatic than Rosa but similarly responds more to the man than to his ideas. René, even before the ill-fated naval expedition, favors a more activist stance than Esteban: "They are all waiting for the miracle of their life. But it is precisely their life that is the great miracle." In the end, it is René's revolutionary position that prevails and triumphs. There is no compromise with a decadent society; one must simply start over.

The initial failure of the youth crusade may be attributed to a lack of unity and direction on the part of the young people. While some members of the church hierarchy, like the king's advisers, wish to oppose them openly, Pope Inocencio predicts that the danger will disappear without his becoming involved: "They themselves and time are their real enemies." Until the final scene of the play, the pope's assessment appears to be correct.

The youth crusade is subject to a certain amount of criticism in the text, but the real object of Salom's satirical barbs is the prevailing society in which they live. Representatives of government, church, business, and society in general are caricatured. When the crusaders are on the way to Marseilles, Esteban's own father tries to exploit the

situation by selling souvenirs. The most exaggerated caricatures of
the play are the two merchants, Hugo el Hierro (the Iron) and
Guillermo el Cerdo (the Pig), creators of the consumer society. They
simultaneously conspire to destroy Esteban and his followers and
urge everyone to buy clothes copied after the youth movement.

As was the case with *Nine Toasts for a King*, the political theme
underlying *The Crusades* is readily apparent from the text, but its
effectiveness in theatrical terms is more dependent upon the actual
staging and the musical score than the message. Quite clearly, *The
Crusades* is intended to be a spectacle on an even larger scale than the
earlier historical farce. Like *Lemon Peel*, it also incorporates some
nudity, a factor which might be expected to attract attention in Spain
where such scenes were prohibited before 1975. From a more literary
point of view, *The Crusades* is important as an indication of Salom's
constantly evolving theater and ideology. It is one more step in a
trajectory that has taken him from a conservative defense of Catholicism to a liberal, even radical, call for change.

III   El corto vuelo del gallo

Following the staging of *Lemon Peel*, Salom became a national
spokesperson for divorce reform. With *The Rooster's Short Flight*, he
again achieved celebrity status. His drama about Francisco Franco's
father Nicolás, which opened on September 18, 1980, in the Es-
pronceda 34 theater, was the immediate source of controversy. Critical reaction was mixed, although the public responded favorably. By
early November Madrid's *Guía del Ocio*, the weekly guide to entertainment in the city, had proclaimed Salom's first play of the new
decade to be "the big hit of the season." The author became the
subject of frequent interviews in newspapers and on radio and television. Popular magazines ranging from *Blanco y Negro* and *Gaceta
Ilustrada* to *Tiempo de Historia* and *Playboy* carried features on the
play and on the Franco family.[15] Pilar Franco, Francisco's sister,
whose own book of memoirs was scheduled for publication in October, reportedly considered suing the author for his negative portrayal both of her father and of her brother Ramón.[16]

Continuing techniques introduced in *Lemon Peel*, *The Rooster's
Short Flight* is an expressionistic and theatricalist play.[17] The action
unfolds on two planes, both of which develop in episodic fashion. The
present or realistic plane begins in 1939, immediately following the

Civil War, and ends in 1942 with Nicolás's death. The second plane is
an evocation of the past through the old man's consciousness as he
recalls real or imaginary scenes with his wife Pilar and their
children—Nicolás, Ramón, and Pilar; Francisco never appears on
stage—from the turn of the century until the beginning of the war.
There is great fluidity of action between one level of reality and the
other. Although the memory/imagination plane is largely a stream-
of-consciousness device reflecting Nicolás's inner world, as in Miller's *Death of a Salesman*, it does not disappear with the death of the
protagonist. Nicolás himself protests the funeral arrangements made
for him by his son Francisco, and Agustina, the woman with whom
Nicolás lived for almost forty years after separating from his wife and
children, is confronted by Pilar, who has been dead for eight years.
Effectively it is Agustina's consciousness that now evokes the fantasy
world. Thus in the final scene of the play, she and Nicolás can relive
the dance where she first met him.

In *Lemon Peel* Salom combined his use of dual planes of reality with
the doubling of one actress in the roles of Juan's daughter and lover.
More innovative than his use of doubling in earlier plays, Salom's
technique in *Lemon Peel* attracted considerable attention and has
very probably had an impact on other Spanish playwrights. Significantly both of Antonio Buero Vallejo's plays staged since then, *La
detonación* [The Shot, 1977] and *Jueces en la noche* [Judges in the
Night, 1979], employ doubling in a comparable manner. In *The
Rooster's Short Flight*, Salom continues his experimentation. The
same actress portrays both of Nicolás's daughters, Pilar and Agustina.
Her dual role both reinforces the blurring of time and identity in the
old man's mind—he also confuses both Pilar and Agustina with
another daughter, Pacita, who died in childhood—and establishes
that the young Agustina was indeed Nicolás's own child and not the
niece of his housekeeper as family tradition later claimed.[18] For the
sake of convenience and economy, several minor male and female
roles are played by one actor and actress. In one case, this doubling is
used as a transitional device between the two temporal planes. The
action moves swiftly from the present, when the old man is sexually
harassing the maid, to a moment perhaps thirty five years earlier
when his children catch him caressing Florita, a young maid to whom
the adolescent Nicolás is also physically attracted. Throughout *The
Rooster's Short Flight*, doubling is used in having the actors portray
the principal characters at different stages in their lives. Like similar

scenes of comic effect in *The Empty Beach* and *Lemon Peel*, the
grown actors assume the roles of children. The actor playing Nicolás
must portray both the eighty year old and his remembered self from
forty years earlier.[19]

The Rooster's Short Flight belongs in the category of nonrepresentational theater not only for the use of doubling and the introduction
of a plane of memory and imagination but also for certain theatricalist
techniques that recall earlier plays of Salom from *Motor Running* to
The Trunk of Disguises, The Night of the Hundred Birds, and *The
Heirs Apparent.* Several of the characters briefly serve a narrative
function, addressing themselves directly to the audience. A sofa in
the apartment of Nicolás and Agustina in 1939 serves as a train
compartment in which Nicolás and Pilar are riding in 1916 when
Francisco has been injured in battle. Agustina objects to intervening
when Nicolás and his children (with an empty chair representing
Francisco) gather for the reading of Pilar's will because she knows
that she has no part to play in that scene.

In many ways *The Rooster's Short Flight* is one of Salom's most
innovative works in its staging techniques and treatment of time. The
commercial success of the play, however, may be attributed largely to
the interest of the subject itself rather than to theatrical merits.
Nicolás Franco, the only man Francisco Franco allegedly feared, was
the antithesis of his son and of the morality imposed on Franco's
Spain. Liberal in his political views, nonconformist in his lifestyle,
and at least verging on the libertine, Nicolás was a potential source of
scandal to his son. For forty years almost no mention was made of his
existence in newspapers, magazines or books, including official biog-
raphies and even a 565-page interview of Francisco Franco. Salom
asserts that if, during the Franco period, people in the street had
been stopped and asked who Franco's father was, they would have
responded in surprise, "Oh, did the General have a father?"[20] Franco's brother Ramón similarly was a possible cause for concern. A great
aviator and therefore at one time a national hero, he was also a
Republican and, like his father, separated from his first wife. His
death in a plane crash after he switched to the Nationalist side in the
Civil War may have been an accident or may have been sabotage. In
revealing intimate secrets of the Franco family, Salom's drama naturally aroused the curiosity of the Spanish audience.

Although Pilar Franco is quoted as being distressed by Salom's
negative treatment of her father, *The Rooster's Short Flight* is a

balanced and indeed sympathetic portrayal of the strong-willed, independent-spirited, and honest old man. As is true of many of the Catalan's plays, such as *Time of Swords, Nine Toasts for a King,* and *Intimate Stories of Paradise,* the drama reflects Salom's careful research. He has clearly fictionalized his material, but the essence of his characterization and of the story of the Franco family is based on the available historical record and personal accounts. Nicolás emerges from Salom's portrait of him as an imperfect human being—a stubborn man with a bad temper whose harsh punishment of Nicolás in particular apparently left permanent psychological scars—but yet a compelling and attractive figure. To Ramón, his favorite son, Nicolás characterizes himself as a blustering rooster who can crow every morning but can barely fly. He loves liberty but finds himself incapable of fighting for it. Nevertheless he dares to stand up and say what he believes, even to the extent of speaking out against Francisco Franco's dictatorship. He refuses to profit from his name or to accept money sent him by his son Nicolás in spite of the relative poverty in which he, Agustina, and their daughter live. His weaknesses notwithstanding, he is a powerful and admirable character, a man who loves life and individual freedom, who remains true to himself, and whose image remains unaffected even by death. Trenas has compared him to the strong patriarchal figures in Eugene O'Neill's *Desire under the Elms* or Tennessee Williams's *Cat on a Hot Tin Roof.*[21]

For Salom the personal story of the Franco family is one of sociological and political significance for Spain. Returning again to the theme of *Lemon Peel,* he emphasizes the unhappy marriage of Nicolás and Pilar, suggesting that they were sexually incompatible as well as diametrically opposed in their religious, political, and moral views. In allying himself with his mother, Francisco Franco determined the pious and puritannical value system that would be imposed upon Spain throughout his years as Chief of State.[22] Nicolás states that the course of history might have been different if Francisco had caroused more and therefore been more human. In Pilar and the son who most resembles her, he finds incarnate "the other Spain," the intransigently conservative faction that spent many years and thousands of lives fighting for Morroco, that started the Civil War, and that executed prisoners after the war, all in the name of God and Country. Given the episodic structure of the play, Salom is able to present moments from the past that not only reveal Nicolás's character and his relationship with his family but also provide the political and historical context.

For the Spanish theatergoer, the historical and biographical aspects of *The Rooster's Short Flight* may be of special interest, but the play's more universal appeal resides in the human drama of Nicolás and Agustina and the psychological development of their characters. Salom, whose own advocacy of divorce reform is well known, is unquestionably aware of the difficulties that the real Nicolás and Agustina must have confronted in defying society's norms. He transcends the mere historical anecdote by creating his fictionalized version of their love story. Like Juan in *Lemon Peel*, Nicolás suffers internal conflicts over separating himself from his children. His hostility toward Francisco and his scorn for Nicolás notwithstanding, he is distressed that they abandon him, and he genuinely grieves at Ramón's death. The emotional price Agustina pays for their irregular relationship is highlighted by her confrontations with Pilar, remembered or imagined, and by the historical fact that her husband's body is forcefully taken from her after his death by Francisco Franco's police. In a scene inspired by Ramón del Valle-Inclán's *Luces de bohemia* [Bohemian Lights], Salom has Agustina try to revive the dead man by showing him a bottle of wine and having their daughter lift her skirts.[23] Her desperate effort to awaken him reflects both her sense of deep loss and her unwillingness to believe that Nicolás's undaunted spirit could be gone. In Salom's play, with its double planes of reality, Nicolás's body may be taken away but he lives on in the consciousness of the woman with whom he shared forty years of his life. The ending is a powerful and poetic portrayal of mutual love and understanding.

CHAPTER 9

Conclusion

W HEN Jaime Salom began his playwrighting career, he did so from a conservative and traditional perspective. His early moralistic dramas were a defense of a rigid Catholicism. His lighter plays—the *sainetes* and comedies based on the format of the detective story—tended to evade social and political questions. Over the years, as his personal viewpoints have undergone a profound transition, his theater has developed into one of social commitment with works of an openly dialectical and testimonial nature. Even prior to these thematic changes, he began exploring new means of expression, moving from conventional realism to an innovative use of theatricalist techniques. Not surprisingly, his theater resists easy classification. Few playwrights, particularly among those who have achieved renown on the commercial Spanish stage, have been so prone to diversification and experimentation, and fewer still have shown such a radical evolution in ideology.

Although Salom has a close familiarity with modern theater, both Spanish and foreign, and from time to time has reflected the influence of writers such as Pirandello, Priestley, Miller, and Brecht, to a large extent he has retained his independence from any one school or current and even from critical and spectator reaction to his works. He has stated that a playwright should not take very seriously either failures or successes. In his own case, he has remained true to his theatrical instincts, even when his plays have been ignored or attacked; but he has also avoided falling into a formula based on duplicating his triumphs. In the chronological order of their stagings, the only two sequential plays that are obviously closely related are *Parcheesi Party* (December, 1965) and its revision *Saturday Night Date* (March, 1967). The poetic fantasy *The Trunk of Disguises* was followed by the moralistic drama *Lack of Evidence*; the intense human drama of the Civil War *The House of the "Chivas,"* by the political allegory *The Heirs Apparent*; the religious-political drama *Time of Swords*, by the historical farce *Nine Toasts for a King*.

In spite of their variety, Salom's plays of the past two decades do reveal certain continuing tendencies and preoccupations. With very few exceptions—*The White Triangle, Emerald Green, Parcheesi Party*—the Catalan has not considered theater to be mere entertainment but rather a means of disturbing and educating his audience. Indeed, the most noticeable weakness in some of his plays has been his inclination to moralize or sermonize too overtly. In his early works, the object of his interrogation and testimony is the individual conscience. Temptation is everywhere, and it is easy to confuse superficial pleasure with happiness. The path of moral wrong leads to self-destruction and to the destruction of others if they, too, lack the inner strength that comes from a deep religious faith. In his later works, Salom's attention has generally shifted to social conscience and his definitions of right and wrong have become less dogmatic, but in a sense he has simply expanded his critical horizon. Those who place their personal power and privilege above the rights of others are not abiding by true Christian principles, even if they purport to represent the Church. The results of an intransigent and immoral system are a decadent society and the destruction of individual liberty. If in the beginning Salom thought he had a simple answer to the problems he posed, in his mature period he has not been so quick to side with a specific cause. At all times, however, he has seen materialism as a negative force and has focused his hope on those who at least try to resist external circumstances in order to maintain personal integrity.

Salom has moved his idealistic search for the good from the personal to the political plane, but he has not lost sight of basic human concerns. Many of his characters, from Flora in *The Message* to Juan in *Lemon Peel*, are anguished individuals striving to give some meaning to their existences. They may err like Adrián (*Lack of Evidence* and *The Night of the Hundred Birds*) in not being content with what they have, or they may learn that fulfillment lies in renunciation and faith, as did Petra (*The House of the "Chivas"*), but in one form or another they ask the eternal question, "What is life?" In a few cases, ranging from the light comedies *Winter Games* and *The Trunk of Disguises* to the allegorical *The Empty Beach,* the emphasis is on the inevitability of death. In almost all cases, the quest for happiness is equated with the need for love. An exceptional character, like Laura in *Mirror for Two Women* or Juan in *The House of the "Chivas,"* can subordinate human love to a religious ideal, but more often Salom depicts the yearning, usually unfulfilled, for a deep relationship that transcends both convenience and passion to reach a level of authentic understanding. Perhaps because Salom regards love as such an essential element of human happiness, he has turned his attention time and time again to marital conflicts.

In some respects, Salom's view of the human condition, both in his moralistic period and in his later works of social commitment, appears pessimistic. With the exception of a few comedies, the marriages he depicts are unsatisfactory ones and love is either unrequited or, like that of Juan and Bárbara in *Lemon Peel*, destroyed by outside forces. On the social and political level, the quest for truth or efforts at reform are generally doomed to failure. Fernando in *The Heirs Apparent* admits defeat and commits suicide. Vallseca in *Nine Toasts for a King* remains true to his convictions but in so doing stands totally alone. The unhappy endings notwithstanding, there is a strong current of optimism underscoring Salom's theater. He maintains his faith in the individual and in his or her desire to change for the better. Initially the theme is expressed in orthodox religious terms, but it is present in the plays of social or political commentary as well, in such characters as Fernando (*The Heirs Apparent*) and Juan (*Lemon Peel*). In essence, Salom's attitude toward his characters is not unlike that of the Angel in *Intimate Stories of Paradise* who shakes his head in dismay at their defects, yet feels compassion and tenderness for humanity. Society is in a state of decline, but there is a hope for the future, particularly if a younger generation is willing to set aside the mistaken value system of the past. *The Heirs Apparent, Nine Toasts for a King*, and especially *The Crusades* offer the possibility, at least, of creating a better world. God may be silent, but He is not dead; Pentecost may yet come.

The trajectory of Salom's theater to some extent parallels the changes that have taken place in Spanish society during the past twenty-five years. His rejection of the rigid conservatism of his youth is consistent with Spain's transition from a totalitarian state to a more open and democratic government. Because his ideology tends to be more liberal than that of the middle class, certainly of his generation, his plays in fact sometimes anticipate the reforms. Although his theater may be seen as a commentary on or a reaction to the situation in his own country, Salom's best works achieve universality. Some of them, such as *The Trunk of Disguises, The Empty Beach*, and *Time of Swords*, are not limited historically or geographically; others, like *The Heirs Apparent, Lemon Peel*, and *The Rooster's Short Flight*, that have a specifically Spanish setting, nevertheless present a level of existential anguish that may be relevant to anyone, anywhere.

Since the late 1960s, Jaime Salom has emerged as one of the leading playwrights on the contemporary Spanish stage. The works with which he has established and reinforced his fame reflect a wide variation in theme and technique. If the Catalan's constant experimentation has not always yielded consistent results, it has helped him develop an unusual versatility. His most significant plays range from poetic fantasy to realistic psychological drama to symbolic tragedy. While it is difficult to predict what new directions he may follow in the 1980s, Salom, now at the height of his creative powers, promises to continue to play an important role in Spanish theater in the years ahead.

Notes and References

Chapter One

1. Personal interview, June 12, 1978. Unless otherwise indicated, all translations to English are my own.

2. Unpublished autobiographical statement, "El autor visto por sí mismo," prepared by Salom in 1976 for an open university radio program, p. 6. Subsequent references to this paper are cited in the text as A.

3. Marqueríe, *Realidad y fantasía en el teatro de Jaime Salom* (Madrid: Escelicer, 1973), pp. 11–12. Subsequent references to this study are cited in the text as Marqueríe.

4. Jaime Delgado, "El teatro de Jaime Salom," in *Teatro selecto de Jaime Salom* (Madrid: Escelicer, 1971), p. ix. Subsequent references to this study are cited in the text as Delgado.

5. José Carol, *Entre la espada y la pared: Interrogatorio a los españoles* (Barcelona: Ediciones Rondas, 1974), p. 258.

6. Ibid., p. 259.

7. Fernando Méndez-Leite, *Historia del cine español*, vol. 2 (Madrid: Rialp, 1965), p. 420.

8. Ibid., pp. 584–85.

9. "Encuesta," *Primer Acto* 29–30 (December, 1961–January, 1962): 13.

10. Marion P. Holt, *The Contemporary Spanish Theater (1949–1972)* (Boston: Twayne, 1975), p. 156. When I mentioned Holt's observation to Salom, he quickly noted the earlier success of fellow Catalan Eduardo Marquina (1879–1946).

11. Sainz de Robles, *Teatro español, 1963–64* (Madrid: Aguilar, 1965), p. 14.

12. Francisco Alvaro, *El espectador y la crítica (El teatro en España en 1967)* (Valladolid: Edición del autor, 1968), p. 369.

13. Ibid., p. 368.

14. Alvaro, *El espectador y la crítica (El teatro en España en 1969)* (Valladolid: Edición del autor, 1970), pp. 333, 348.

15. J.E. Aragonés, "Teatro," *La Estafeta Literaria* 396 (May 18, 1968): 31.

16. In our interview of June 12, 1978, Salom attributed the failure of the Moratín to the lack of theatrical tradition in Barcelona. His assessment of the situation in Barcelona is one frequently made by commentators on the Spanish stage who note that theatrical activity continues to be centralized in Madrid. Salom discussed his problems as an impressario in more detail in an

141

interview with Lolita Sánchez published in *Tele eXprés*, Barcelona, February 17, 1972.

17. Personal interview, June 12, 1978. Salom wrote *La casa de las Chivas* in 1964 so that it represents his attitude at that period, not the late 1960s.

18. Ansón, "Prólogo" to *Teatro/Jaime Salom* (Madrid: G. del Toro, 1974), p. 11.

19. Ibid., p. 15.

20. *La piel del limón* (Madrid: Escelicer, 1976), p. 21. Subsequent references are to this edition and are cited in the text as *L*.

21. Personal interview, June 12, 1978.

22. Ibid. Although in 1976 some critics in Spain thought divorce reform was an outdated topic because of the change in government, in late 1980 there was still no divorce law and the debate therefore continued. See Jaime Salom, "Jaime Salom entrevista a Francisco Fernández Ordóñez: El divorcio se produce cuando la vida familiar se ha hecho imposible," *Nueva*, November, 1980, pp. 10–16.

23. The subject is analyzed in some depth in Jöelle Brunel, "Les personnages féminins dans l'oeuvre de Jaime Salom" (M.A. thesis, Université Paul Valéry, Montpellier, France, 1975).

24. Personal interview, June 16, 1978.

25. Personal interview, June 12, 1978.

26. Salom, "La dura piel del matrimonio," *Yes*, March 1977, p. 23.

27. Salom, "La teología radica en el teatro," in Marqueríe, p. 28.

28. Salom, "¿Quién decís que soy yo?" *Jesucristo* 10 (1974): 38.

29. *Ideologías para un rey*, 2d. ed. (Madrid: Editoria Aguaribay, 1975), p. 46.

30. Personal letter dated March 18, 1978. *Ankylotic*, the adjective Salom uses to describe his former orthodox Catholicism, is a medical term referring to the abnormal adhesion of bones to a joint. It is an expressive way of indicating rigidity and immobility.

31. Personal interview, June 12, 1978.

32. Marqueríe mentions both of these interests (p. 13).

33. Personal interview, June 12, 1978.

34. Carol, p. 260.

Chapter Two

1. Beatriz Iraburu, "Jaime Salom y su coloquio frustrado en Pamplona," *Diario de Navarra*, May 13, 1975, p. 24.

2. Angel Laborda, "Jaime Salom: En España no se ha superado el miedo a la libertad," *Blanco y Negro*, December 13, 1975, p. 90.

3. Carol, p. 258.

4. Personal interview, June 12, 1978.

5. This paragraph and the following one are based on Marqueríe, pp. 47–54.

6. Personal interview, June 12, 1978.

7. I am indebted to Jaime Salom for making these manuscripts as well as those of several other later unpublished plays available to me.

8. "La hora gris," unpublished manuscript, act 1. The manuscript pages are not numbered.

9. Quoted by Salom in *A*, 17.

10. Holt, p. 156.

11. I will analyze this play and the other published works in later chapters. In that the unpublished plays will not be subject to further discussion, I have included brief plot summaries for them in this chapter.

12. Personal interview, June 12, 1978.

13. Ibid. Salom discusses his attitudes towards the use of Catalan and the presence of biculturalism in Cataluña in "Encuesta con los dramaturgos catalanes que escriben en castellano," *Estreno*, 5, no. 2 (Fall, 1979): 12–13.

14. Holt, p. 156.

15. Personal interview, June 12, 1978.

16. Ibid.

17. "Encuesta," p. 13.

18. Ruiz Iriarte's *pobrecito* is a character whose appearance and manner are unassuming and whose inner worth is therefore often overlooked. In several of his comedies, such as *El aprendiz de amante*, *Juego de niños*, *La soltera rebelde*, and *El pobrecito embustero*, the character deliberately plays a role in order to help himself or someone else achieve love or happiness.

19. Holt, p. 156.

20. Personal letter dated November 23, 1978.

21. Salom does not remember the titles of all of the several scripts he worked on in the late 1950s and early 1960s nor does he consider this an important aspect of his literary career. This particular script is the only one available at the Biblioteca Nacional in Madrid.

22. Iraburu, p. 24.

23. Personal interview, June 12, 1978.

24. Muñiz, "*La casa de las Chivas*," *Tele/radio* 1065 (May 22–28, 1978): 16.

25. Personal interview, June 12, 1978. Salom's favorite plays in order of preference are *Tiempo de espadas*, *Los delfines*, *La piel del limón*, *La playa vacía*, and *El baúl de los disfraces*. Significantly, each of these plays is quite distinct in theme and technique from the other four. Salom has stated that "the authentic success in art cannot be repeated," and it is perhaps for this reason that he has not tried to duplicate any of his own major works. See Salom, "Prólogo" to Alvaro, *El espectador y la crítica* (*El teatro en España en 1974*) (Madrid: Prensa Española, 1975), p. ix.

26. Holt, p. 158.

27. The lecture appears in Marquerie, pp. 27–46.

28. Pilar Urbano, "Jaime Salom: Espadas de doble filo," *Diario de Lérida*, October 13, 1973, p. 12.

29. Ansón, p. 14.

30. Alvaro, *El espectador y la crítica (El teatro en España en 1973)* (Madrid: Prensa Española, 1974), p. 204.

31. Personal interview, June 12, 1978.

32. Perico Pomar, "El teatro comercial español está a nivel europeo," *Diario de Mallorca,* October 30, 1975, p. 17.

33. Personal letter, November 4, 1978.

34. Personal letters, November 4, 1978, and January 30, 1979.

35. Personal interview, June 16, 1978.

36. Sagarra, "Jaime Salom: El día de siempre," *Tele eXprés,* January 26, 1970.

37. Pomar, p. 17. Paso's prolific output of light comedies has been considered the epitome of commercial theater in Madrid.

38. Urbano, p. 12.

39. Salom, "Azorín. Hombre de teatro," *Letras de Deusto* 4, no. 7 (1974): 147.

40. Ibid., p. 152.

41. Personal interview, June 16, 1978.

42. Interview in *La prensa,* January 5, 1971.

43. A. P., "Jaime Salom: Oftalmólogo en ejercicio activo y empresario teatral," *Bierro,* September 22, 1971.

44. Pablo Cistue de Castro has identified Buero, Salom and Gala as the three most important playwrights in contemporary Spain ("Genealidad de un dramaturgo y magisterio de un crítico," *Heraldo de Aragón,* March 14, 1974). Pablo G. del Barco attributes the only real attempt at creating theater to Gala, Salom, Martínez Mediero and a few younger playwrights whose works have been suppressed ("¿Cuándo un Ministerio de Cultura?" *El Europeo,* August 16, 1975, p. 24).

45. Guillermo Díaz-Plaja, "¿Qué es la creación literaria?" *ABC,* May 3, 1970, p. 31.

Chapter Three

1. A number of critics have noted the impact of Christie or Priestley on certain Spanish playwrights. See, for example, Marquerie, *Veinte años de teatro en España* (Madrid: Editora Nacional, 1959), p. 153; Gonzalo Torrente Ballester, *Panorama de la literatura española contemporánea, vol. 2, 2d ed. (Madrid: Guadarrama, 1961), p. 576; John C. Dowling, "The Theater of Alfonso Paso," Modern Language Journal* 45 (1961): 196.

2. *Verde esmeralda* will be considered in chapter 4.

3. Alvaro, *El espectador y la crítica (El teatro en España en 1973),* p. 220.

4. Review from *Nuevo Diario* excerpted in Alvaro, *El espectador y la crítica (El teatro en Espana en 1972)* (Madrid: Prensa Española, 1973), p. 169.

5. Ibid., pp. 168, 273.

6. Holt suggests such an influence on Ruiz Iriarte's *El carrusell* (1964) where a commissioner, who functions as conscience, comes to hear a confession concerning the suicide of a young woman (p. 105). Similarly, a mysterious judge hears three confessions in José María Pemán's *Tres testigos* (1970).

7. Marquerie points out that the "personaje eludido," a character who is mentioned but never appears, may be traced back to Terence and Roman comedy; he also notes the example of the imaginary title character in López Rubio's *Alberto* (p. 59).

8. There are a number of interesting parallels in plot and characterization between *El mensaje* and Elena Quiroga's first novel *La soledad sonora* [Sonorous Solitude, 1949]. In the novel Elisa genuinely believes that her husband Diego, whom she does not really love, has died on the Russian front before she marries José, whom she loves deeply. When Diego returns, she elects to live alone with her memories.

9. Marquerie suggests the possible influence of Priestley and of Arthur Miller on Salom's use of time in *Falta de pruebas* and *La noche de los cien pájaros* (p. 142). Miller's *Death of a Salesman*, which incorporates two planes of reality and retrospective scenes, was first staged in Madrid in 1952 and has had a notable impact on Spanish theater.

10. *Falta de pruebas* opened in Barcelona on September 16, 1964. *El carrusell* premiered the following December 4 in Madrid. It is therefore unlikely that there is a direct influence of Salom's play on Ruiz Iriarte's work.

11. Salom's knowledge as a doctor is apparent here as in the exhumation and subsequent autopsy in *Culpables*.

12. Carolina spends time in a mental home because of her nervous reaction to Rogelio's infidelity. Although Salom was still strongly opposed to divorce when he wrote *Falta de pruebas*, the play reveals a deteriorated marriage not unlike that of Juan and Rosa in *La piel del limón*.

13. "Autocrítica" to *Falta de pruebas* (Madrid: Escelicer, 1968), p. 5.

14. *La noche de los cien pájaros* (Madrid: Escelicer, 1972), p. 18. Subsequent references to this play are cited in the text as *N*.

15. Prego, review from *ABC* reprinted in Sainz de Robles, ed., *Teatro español, 1971–1972* (Madrid: Aguilar, 1973), p. 176.

16. Ibid.

17. Lázaro Carreter, review from *Gaceta Illustrada* excerpted in Alvaro, *El espectador y la crítica (El teatro en España en 1972)*, p. 7.

Chapter Four

1. I am excluding from this group *El baúl de los disfraces*, a major play also staged in January, 1964. I have classified it as a work of poetic fantasy and will consider it in chapter 5.

2. María Victoria Morales mentions three plays of Jardiel and six of Paso in her discussion of the police comedy. See "The Farcical Mode in the Spanish Theater of the Twentieth Century" (Ph.D. diss., Columbia University, 1969), pp. 116–120. See also my "Macabre Humor in the Contemporary Spanish Theater," *Romance Notes* 9 (1968): 201–5.

3. *Verde esmeralda* (Madrid: Escelicer, 1962), p. 27.

4. José María Junyent, review from *El Correo Catalán* excerpted in *La gran aventura* (Barcelona: Editorial Millà, 1963), p. 62.

5. See discussion of *Falta de pruebas* in chapter 3. Olmo's introduction of simultaneous action in *La camisa* slightly antedates Salom's use of this technique.

6. "Autocrítica" to *Juegos de invierno* (Madrid: Escelicer, 1964), p. 5. Subsequent references to this play are cited in the text as *W*.

7. See Alvaro, *El espectador y la crítica (El teatro en España en 1964)* (Valladolid: Edición del autor, 1965), pp. 24–26.

Chapter Five

1. Personal letter, March 18, 1978.

2. Theatricalist or nonrepresentational theater rejects realism, that is, the effort to create the illusion that what is happening on stage is real life. For a brief overview of theatricalism see Edward Mabley, "Appendix B: The Revolt Against Realism," in his *Dramatic Construction: An Outline of Basic Principles* (Philadelphia: Chilton, 1972), pp. 413–21.

3. Review from *Gaceta Ilustrada*, quoted in Alvaro, *El espectador y la crítica (El teatro en España en 1964)*, p. 104.

4. *El baúl de los disfraces* in *Teatro selecto de Jaime Salom*, p. 144. Subsequent references are to this edition and are cited in the text as *T*.

5. "Autocrítica" to *El baúl de los disfraces*, in *Teatro español, 1963–1964*, p. 317.

6. *The Happy Journey* . . . was published in 1931 in the The *Long Christmas Day and Other Plays*. For an introduction to Wilder's theatricalist theater, see Rex Burbank, *Thornton Wilder* (New York: Twayne, 1961).

7. Marquerie mentions in passing a possible relationship between *El baúl de los disfraces* and Evreinov's *La comedia de la felicidad* without specifying the points of comparison (p. 247).

8. Review from *Pueblo* quoted by Alvaro, *El espectador y la crítica (El teatro en España en 1965)* (Valladolid: Edición del autor, 1966), p. 172.

9. Review from *ABC* quoted by Alvaro, ibid., and by Marquerie, p. 264.

10. The reconciliation of the married couple here foreshadows a similar situation in *La piel del limón*.

11. Jerzy Grotowski, founder of The Polish Lab Theater in 1959, is a proponent of staging that seeks to define what is distinctively theatrical. Because Salom continues to use lights, sound, and to some extent costumes

and scenery, he has not reduced *Cita los sábados* to the interaction of actors and audience that Grotowski's concept of "poor theater" implies when fully implemented.

12. The exception is the third episode which begins the second act.

13. The one basic change is the reversal in roles of Felipe and Agapito, the former now portraying Leoncia's lover rather than the beggar.

14. According to Marqueríe, Salom's use of circus terminology is inaccurate (pp. 299–300). The authenticity of the background is, however, of little importance to the play as a whole.

15. *Viaje en un trapecio*, in *Teatro selecto de Jaime Salom*, p. 464. Subsequent references are to this edition and are cited in the text as *V*.

16. "Autocrítica," quoted by Marqueríe, pp. 297–98.

17. Martínez Tomás, review quoted by Alvaro, *El espectador y la crítica (El teatro en España en 1970)* (Madrid: Prensa Española, 1971), p. 351.

18. Reminiscent of the *Odioso Señor* in Mihura's *Tres sombreros de copa*, Schmitt's pockets are filled with gifts to be used for the purpose of seduction.

19. Marqueríe compares this scene to a moment in Fernando Arrabal's *El arquitecto y el emperador de Asiria* (p. 307). Although the tone and intention of the two plays are quite different, they are related in their extensive use of role-playing and their theatricalist techniques.

Chapter Six

1. Salom mentioned the influence of Chekhov on *Espejo para dos mujeres* in our interview of June 16, 1978. Priestley refers to the influence of the Russian playwright on his *Eden End* and *The Linden Tree* in the introduction to *The Plays of J. B. Priestley*, vol. 1 (London: William Heinemann, 1948), p. xviii.

2. *Espejo para dos mujeres* (Madrid: Escelicer, 1966), p. 46. Subsequent references are to this edition and are cited in the text as *M*.

3. These are opinions expressed in reviews from *Marca*, *ABC*, and *Ya*, respectively. See Alvaro, *El espectador y la crítica (El teatro en España en 1965)*, pp. 162–66.

4. Personal interview, June 12, 1978. Ideas attributed to Salom in the paragraph that follows are also from this interview.

5. José Corrales Egea identifies the period of demythification in the novel to be 1965–1970. See *La novela española actual* (Madrid: Cuadernos para el Diálogo, 1971), pp. 158–75.

6. A. Martínez Tomás, review from *La Vanguardia* reprinted in Sainz de Robles, *El teatro español, 1967–1968* (Madrid: Aguilar, 1969), p. 243.

7. "Autocrítica" to *La casa de las Chivas*, in Sainz de Robles, *Teatro español, 1967–1968*, p. 239.

8. *La casa de las Chivas*, in *Teatro Selecto de Jaime Salom*, p. 240. Subsequent references are to this edition and are cited in the text as *H*.

9. Alvaro, *El espectador y la crítica (El teatro en España en 1969)*, p. 3.

10. Delgado, in his otherwise excellent introduction to *La casa de las Chivas*, suggests that Petra is a "purely existentialist" character who gives herself to men for her own pleasure (p. xxxiv). Aside from his erroneous use of the term existentialist, I believe he has misunderstood Petra's characterization.

11. Marquerie reports an interesting round-table discussion organized by Luis María Ansón in which the participants offered varying opinions on the principal characters, their motivation, and their responsibility (pp. 182–84).

12. Salom does not specify the ages of the various soldiers, but presumably Juan is younger than the other men but more attractive to Trini than the boyish *Nene*.

13. The leftist political parties were in diametrical opposition to the Catholic Church. In Republican-held territory, religious institutions were closed; priests and nuns were forced into hiding. Juan is therefore unable to declare openly his own beliefs and vocation. Part of Salom's purpose in writing *La casa de las Chivas* is to reject the notion that all those who fought on the Republican side were necessarily anticlerical.

14. Luis Marsillach, review from *Diario de Barcelona*, reprinted in *Teatro español, 1967–1968*, p. 241.

15. In that Salom has now repudiated other positions of the Catholic Church that differ from more general Christian beliefs, he probably sees no reason for priests to be celibate.

16. See, for example, Luis Molero Manglano, *Teatro Español contemporáneo* (Madrid: Editora Nacional, 1974), p. 330; Marquerie, p. 181.

17. One of the first treatments of the subject, actually antedating the tourist invasion, is Mercedes Salisachs' *Una mujer llega al pueblo* (1957).

18. *La playa vacía*, in *Teatro selecto de Jaime Salom*, pp. 324–25. Subsequent references are to this edition and are cited in the text as *E*.

19. In Spanish, Victoria and life (*vida*) share a common initial letter as do Pablo and pleasure (*placer*).

20. Salom does not number the scenes but indicates breaks in the action through moments of darkness. In this manner he divides each of the two acts into three scenes.

21. For a detailed analysis of the four characters, see Delgado (xlvi–lvii; reprinted as "Prólogo" to *La playa vacía* and *Tiempo de espadas* [Madrid: Espasa-Calpe, 1975], pp. 13–22).

22. Lorenzo López Sancho has suggested that Salom's vision of death is inspired by the Austrian poet Rainer Maria Rilke (1875–1926): review from *ABC* reprinted in *Teatro español, 1970–1971* (Madrid: Aguilar, 1972), p. 160. One might as easily seek Hispanic sources, such as Seneca, who lived in the Iberian peninsula, or the modern Spanish philosopher Miguel de Unamuno (1864–1936). Certainly Victoria's existential anguish is closely related to Unamuno's tragic sense of life.

23.   Alvaro believes that this last scene is unnecessary and weakens the play's effectiveness: *El espectador y la crítica (El teatro en España en 1970)*, p. 132. I am inclined to disagree with this opinion as well as with three critics quoted by Alvaro who felt that the play was not poetic enough or not well structured (ibid, pp. 134, 136). As reported by Alvaro, critical reaction to *La playa vacía* was mixed.

24.   López Sancho, p. 160. Significantly, two of the critics quoted by Alvaro as having a negative reaction to Salom's play—Carlos Luis Alvarez of *Arriba* and Antonio Valencia of *Marca*—are also among those making the comparison with Casona. López Sancho suggests that *La playa vacía* might better be compared with Azorín's more experimental trilogy *Lo invisible* (1927–1928). While this suggestion has a certain validity, the actual points of contact between the Salom and Azorín plays are superficial and are largely limited to the third play of the trilogy, *Doctor Death, de 3 a 5*.

25.   Salom originally intended to use an actual paddle boat but in the Madrid production a rope, presumably tied to the boat, was substituted (*E*, 380).

26.   Marqueríe divides Salom's theater into "obras a noticia" ("realistic works") and "obras a fantasía" ("poetic works"). He classifies *La playa vacía* in the latter group with the four plays I have considered in chapter 5.

27.   All three reviews reprinted in *Teatro español, 1970–1971* are favorable ones (pp. 160–65).

28.   Review excerpted in *El espectador y la crítica (El teatro en España en 1970)*, p. 134.

29.   Rotellar, review reprinted in *Teatro español, 1970–1971*, p. 163.

30.   Some critics have failed to realize that only Victoria is portrayed as a real human being and hence mortal. The most curious comment along this line is that of José María Claver who says that all four characters "are going to the sea of death" (review excerpted in *El espectador y la crítica [El teatro en España en 1970]*, p. 133).

31.   In his self-criticism of the play, Salom makes precisely this point: "But perhaps also—and this is what moved me to write this story of life, death, sex and love—in solitude and silence, someone will rethink those tormenting problems that have no human solution, no purely natural explanation, but that the mere sincerity of posing them, face to face, contains within itself a small germ of hope" (*Teatro español, 1970–1971*, pp. 159–60).

Chapter Seven

1.   Although most critics had high praise for Burman's stage setting, Alvaro remarks that he preferred a production in Valladolid that was done with simple black curtains and no set. He found that the bare stage allowed him to follow the nuances of the dialogue better. See *El espectador y la crítica (El teatro en España en 1969)*, p. 122.

2. Salom, "Autocrítica" to *Los delfines*, in Sainz de Robles, *Teatro español, 1968–1969* (Madrid: Aguilar, 1970), p. 235.

3. Not surprisingly, the theme of the "generación puente" and the generation gap received extensive treatment in the novel before the theater. See, for example, chapter 13 of Elena Quiroga's *La careta* (1955).

4. Salom, "El autor visto por sí mismo," pp. 29, 31. The interview Salom excerpts here appeared in *La Vanguardia.*

5. *Los delfines*, in *Teatro selecto de Jaime Salom.* Subsequent references are to this edition and are cited in the text as *D.* Dauphin was the title given to the heir to the French throne from 1349 to 1830.

6. *Teatro español, 1968–1969*, p. 236.

7. I am relying for the description of the setting on the reviews excerpted by Alvaro in *El espectador y la crítica (El teatro en España en 1969)*, pp. 121–22.

8. Marqueríe, whose analysis of *Los delfines* is one of the most useful studies in his book on Salom's theater, praises this use of Fernando as narrator as being a less artificial device than the Stage Manager in *Our Town* (p. 204). Both techniques are, of course, theatricalist ones.

9. David Ladra, "Objetividad y universalidad versus realidad," *Primer Acto* 113 (October, 1969): p. 67; Molero Manglano, p. 332.

10. Elías Gómez Picazo, review from *Madrid* excerpted in *El espectador y la críticia (El teatro en España en 1969)*, p. 123.

11. Juan Emilio Aragonés, *Teatro español de posguerra* (Madrid: Publicaciones Españolas, 1971), p. 71; Molero Manglano, p. 332. Even critics praising the play, such as Julio Manegat, suggest that in some scenes the rhythm is too slow (*Teatro español, 1968–1969*, p. 240). Having not seen the play staged, I am unable to reach a judgment of my own on this aspect of its theatrical effectiveness.

12. Ladra, p. 66.

13. José María Claver, review from *Ya*, in *El espectador y la crítica (El teatro en España en 1969)*, p. 123; Antonio Valencia, review from *Marca*, ibid., p. 125.

14. As noted in chapter 1, Luis María Ansón believes that Salom's shift to plays of denunciation provoked deliberate attacks on his theater from Madrid intellectuals, who had previously not taken him very seriously. See Ansón, "Prólogo" to *Teatro/Jaime Salom*, p. 11

15. I find the ending to be deliberately ambiguous and therefore disagree with Marqueríe's opinion that Fere's final "never . . . , never . . . , never. . . ." implies a definitive break with the past (pp. 199–200). In terms of the specific parallels between the play and Spanish history, it is worthy of note that in 1969 Juan Carlos was named Franco's heir. The middle generation—the future king's father—was thus eliminated from possible succession just as Fernando eventually is.

16. Unlike realistic or psychological drama, in tragedy characters do tend to be two-dimensional. As J. L. Styan observes, "The farther drama leans towards farce or tragedy, the more the actor assumes the 'mask'." See *Drama, Stage and Audience* (London: Cambridge University Press, 1975), p. 82.

17. Obviously I am in disagreement with Molero Manglano who sees Susana as one of the "two and a half doors to hope" for the future. Raúl is the other full door while Mara, whose rebellion takes the form of sexual freedom and travel abroad, is the half door. See Molero Manglano, p. 334.

18. Morales, review from *Diario de Barcelona* reprinted in *Teatro español, 1968–1969*, p. 243.

19. Luciano del Río, "Desde Barcelona: Entrevista con Jaime Salom acerca de 'Tiempo de espadas,'" *Diario de Pontevedra*, March 14, 1974.

20. Salom, "El autor visto por sí mismo," p. 34.

21. Marqueríe connects *Tiempo de espadas* with Jerzy Grotowski not only for the almost bare stage but also for the coincidental similarity of theme treated by the Polish playwright in *Apocalipsis cum figuris*, (1972).

22. While Salom's reasons for not attempting to portray Christ are readily apparent, it should be noted that the playwright has built several of his plays from *El mensaje* to *Los delfines* around a character who never appears on stage, a "personaje eludido" in Marqueríe's terminology.

23. Interview with José Antonio Flaquer from *El Noticiero Universal* (June 6, 1973), excerpted in Sainz de Robles, *Teatro español, 1972–1973* (Madrid: Aguilar, 1974), p. 78. Salom did not write an *autocrítica* of this play; accordingly, Sainz de Robles quotes extensively from several interviews, some of which also appear in Marqueríe's book.

24. Salom, *Tiempo de espadas*, in *La playa vacía* and *Tiempo de espadas* (Madrid: Espasa-Calpe, 1975), p. 157. Subsequent references are to this edition and are cited in the text as S.

25. Urbano, interview in *Telva* (May 15, 1973), reprinted as "Jaime Salom: Espadas de doble filo," *Diario de Lérida*, October 13, 1973, p. 12.

26. Interview with Angel Laborda in *ABC* (September 28, 1972), excerpted in *Teatro español, 1972–1973*, p. 77.

27. Interview with Soraya in *Pueblo* (September 30, 1972), quoted by Marqueríe, p. 220.

28. Soraya interview in Marqueríe, p. 221.

29. Interview with Isabel Sancho in *Crítica* (April, 1973), excerpted in *Teatro español, 1972–1973*, p. 76.

30. Ansón, p. 14.

31. Alfonso de Castro in *ABC*, quoted by Marqueríe, p. 241.

32. Andrés Berlanga, "Jaime Salom: 9 brindis por un rey," *El Correo Catalán* (Barcelona), November 3, 1974, p. 15.

33. Salom, "El autor visto por sí mismo," p. 39.

34. Berlango; and Salom, "La lección de Caspe," in *Nueve brindis por un rey* (Madrid: Escelicer, 1975), pp. 7–8. References to the play are to this edition and are cited in the text as *B*.

35. Pilar Trenas, "'Nueve brindis por un rey', teatro vivo," *ABC Reportaje*, November 1, 1974.

36. Ibid.

37. Ibid. The following spring when *Nueve brindis por un rey* was staged in Pamplona, the municipal government failed to give permission for a round table discussion in which the author was to participate, and the meeting had to be canceled. See Beatriz Iraburu, "Jaime Salom y su coloquio frustrado en Pamplona," *Diario de Navarra*, May 13, 1975, p. 24.

38. Aragonés, review from *La Estafeta Literaria* excerpted in Alvaro, *El espectador y la crítica (El teatro en España en 1974)* (Madrid: Prensa Española, 1975), p. 89.

39. According to Alberto de la Hera, the censors substituted cricket for golf, a change he labels one of the most ridiculous in recent years. See "Nueve brindis para [*sic*] un rey," *Primer Acto* 177 (February, 1975) 62. Among several short scenes and passages suppressed in the Madrid production were two critical reactions to the senseless loss of human life at the battle of Murverdre. Presumably the golf clubs were seen as a direct satire on contemporary politicians while the latter scenes were viewed as antipatriotic.

40. Typical of the negative response to Vergel's direction was Adolfo Prego's comment that the text and the staging seemed unrelated. See "Nueve brindis por un rey," *ABC* (October 1, 1974), p. 77. Positive comments on the stagings are quoted in Alvaro, *El espectador y la crítica (El teatro en España en 1974)*, pp. 91–92.

41. De la Hera goes so far as to say that few spectators will know anything at all about Caspe (p. 62).

42. Enrique Llovet, who did not like *La piel del limón*, did praise Salom for writing an emotional drama rather than continuing in the vogue of Brechtian epic theater. See Alvaro, *El espectador y la crítica (El teatro en España en 1976)* (Madrid: Prensa Espanola, 1977), p. 70.

43. In Spanish, because of the feminine form of the pronoun "them" (*ellas*) the two questions are closer than in English.

44. Both M. Diez Crespo and Aragonés point out this weakness in the play. See *El espectador y la crítica (El teatro en España en 1976)*, pp. 69, 72.

45. With respect to *Los delfines*, Marqueríe observes that Salom introduces suicide as a theme in at least seven of his plays up through *Tiempo de espadas* (p. 213).

Chapter Eight

1. Lluís Bonet Mojica, "Jaime Salom: En esta comedia abordo el tema

feminista con respecto, simpatía y humildad"," *La Vanguardia*, October 4, 1978.

2. Personal interview, June 12, 1978.

3. Bonet Mojica, loc. cit.; "El tema del divorcio, planteado en una obra de Salom, a la Constitución," *El Noticiero*, December 7, 1978, p. 6; Angel Cuevas, "Jaime Salom y sus historias del paraíso," *La Prensa*, November 25, 1978, p. 13. Paradoxically Article 14 of the constitution does contain an equal rights statement which specifically includes sex while Article 57 establishes the concept of male succession to the throne.

4. Theodor Reik, "La creación de la mujer" quoted on the playbill for *Historias íntimas del paraíso*.

5. "Numeri Rabba" as recounted by Robert Graves in *Hebrew Myths* and quoted on playbill.

6. Salom defines his dual purpose—entertaining his audience and making them think—in the "Antecrítica" included on the playbill.

7. *Historias íntimas del paraíso*, unpublished manuscript, act 1, pp. 4–5. Subsequent references are to the manuscript and are cited in the text as *P*. Here, as elsewhere in the text, translations are my own. In 1980, after the manuscript of this book was complete, Marion P. Holt prepared an excellent translation of *Historias íntimas del paraíso* with the title *Behind the Scenes in Eden*. The translation is as yet unpublished. There are as yet no published translations of Salom's theater in English, but English translations are in progress or have been considered of *La casa de las Chivas, Tiempo de espadas*, and *El corto vuelo del gallo*.

8. Personal letter, dated November 4, 1978.

9. Angel Cuevas, p. 13. In this regard it is interesting to note that Simone de Beauvoir's *Le Deuxième sexe* was prohibited in Spain until 1966.

10. Personal letter, November 23, 1978.

11. Bonet Mojica.

12. Andrés Berlanga, "Jaime Salom: 9 brindis por un rey," *El Correo Catalán*, Barcelona, November 3, 1974, p. 15.

13. Angel Cuevas, p. 13.

14. I am indebted to Jaime Salom for allowing me to read a draft of *Las cruzadas* in June, 1978. Because this was not the final version of the script, I shall not discuss the play in detail.

15. Personal letter, November, 1980.

16. Trini de León-Sotelo, "Pilar Franco: '¿Cómo ver la obra sin liarse a tiros?'" *Blanco y Negro*, October 1–7, 1980, p. 16. For the colloquium honoring the 100th performance of the play, Pilar Franco was invited to be one of the participants. She declined, but the playwright and producer sent her a bouquet of flowers. (Julio Trenas, "Un interesante experimento de 'participación teatral': Coloquio en la cien representación de 'El corto vuelo del gallo,'" *La Vanguardia*, November 14, 1980.) Apparently no further mention has been made of a potential lawsuit.

17. I am grateful to the playwright for providing me with a copy of the unpublished manuscript. At the time of this writing, *El corto vuelo del gallo* is scheduled for publication by Grijalbo with an introduction by the historian Rafael Abella. Abella is also the author of the article on Nicolás Franco and Salom's play in the January, 1981, issue of *Tiempo de Historia*, pp. 54–57.

18. Subsequent to the staging of *El corto vuelo del gallo*, Salom received a number of communications from people who knew Nicolás Franco and Agustina. Through these new sources he has learned that Agustina was a schoolteacher, not a maid or seamstress's daughter as he had earlier believed, and that the child who lived with the couple was in fact Agustina's niece as the Franco family claimed. (Trenas, "Un interesante experimento. . . .")

19. In the Madrid production, Andrés Mejuto played Nicolás. According to Trenas, the role was the best performance of the actor's career. " 'El corto vuelo del gallo,' éxito resonante de Jaime Salom," *La Vanguardia*, September 20, 1980, p. 33.) Other members of the cast included Gemma Cuervo as Pilar and María Luisa Merlo as Agustina. The director was Manuel Manzaneque and the stage designer, Wolfgang Burman.

20. Salom, "Nicolás, el padre de los Franco," *Playboy* (Spanish edition), (December, 1980), p. 92.

21. Trenas, " 'El corto vuelo del gallo' . . ." and *Blanco y Negro*, "Retrato de un desconocido: Nicolás, padre de Franco," *Blanco y Negro*, October 1–7, 1980, p. 14.

22. Salom points out that the Franco government not only repealed the divorce law instituted during the Second Republic but also nullified any second marriages during that period. Thus if Nicolás married Agustina after Pilar's death in 1934 as Salom conjectures he might have, given that they had been living together since 1907, the postwar law withdrew recognition from that marriage. (Salom, "Nicolás, el padre de los Franco," p. 140.) The implication is that Franco may have adopted an anti-divorce stand because of siding with his mother in his parents' marital dispute. Similarly there are those who say that Franco attacked Masons because his father was one. ("El padre de Franco, llevado a la escena por Andrés Mejuto," *El Periódico*, Barcelona, December 12, 1980.)

23. In the Valle-Inclán play, the thirteenth scene includes the grotesque efforts to awaken the corpse by those who have joined Max Estrella's grieving widow and daughter. Salom's scene does not have the same quality as the *esperpento*, in large part because it is Agustina herself who desperately wants Nicolás to be alive. Nevertheless, there is some resemblance between the two scenes. Max Estrella and Nicolás are both strong, nonconformist figures. Max's widow and daughter are unable to survive without him and commit suicide. Agustina and her daughter are similarly left without protection; what happens to them historically after Nicolás dies is unknown.

Selected Bibliography

PRIMARY SOURCES

1. Original Plays (In order of performance. Premieres for Barcelona and Madrid are cited for works produced in those cities.)

El mensaje. Bilbao, May 14, 1955; Barcelona, November 13, 1959.

El triángulo blanco. Barcelona, December 2, 1960.

Verde esmeralda. Madrid, December 22, 1960.

Culpables. Madrid, August 8, 1961.

La gran aventura. Barcelona, November 24, 1961.

El cuarto jugador. Lérida, October 5, 1962.

El baúl de los disfraces. Barcelona, January 2, 1964; Madrid, September 29, 1964.

Juegos de invierno. Madrid, January 31, 1964.

Falta de pruebas. Barcelona, September 16, 1964.

Espejo para dos mujeres. Barcelona, September 20, 1965; Madrid, November 30, 1965.

Parchís Party. Madrid, December 4, 1965.

Cita los sábados. Barcelona, March 23, 1967; Madrid, October 1, 1973.

La casa de las Chivas. Barcelona, March 22, 1968; Madrid, January 10, 1969.

Los delfines. Barcelona, January 31, 1969; Madrid, October 1, 1969.

La playa vacía. Madrid, November 20, 1970; Barcelona, February 17, 1971.

Viaje en un trapecio. Barcelona, November 27, 1970.

La noche de los cien pájaros. Madrid, February 10, 1972; Barcelona, September 21, 1973.

Tiempo de espadas. Madrid, September 27, 1972; Barcelona, October 30, 1973.

Nueve brindis por un rey. Madrid, September 27, 1974.

La piel del limón. Madrid, September 10, 1976.

Historias íntimas del paraíso. Madrid, October 6, 1978.

El corto vuello del gallo. Madrid, September 18, 1980.

2. Adaptations

Max Frisch. *La muralla china.* Madrid, January 22, 1971.

Brendan Behan. *El rehén.* Madrid, December 14, 1973.

3. Collections of Plays by Salom

Teatro/Jaime Salom. Madrid: G. del Toro, 1974. "Colección El Autor Imprescindible." Includes *Culpables, El baúl de los disfraces, Espejo para dos*

*mujeres, Cita los sábados, La casa de las Chivas, Los delfines, La playa
vacía, Viaje en un trapecio, La noche de los cien pájaros, Tiempo de
espadas.*
Teatro selecto de Jaime Salom. Madrid: Escelicer, 1971. Includes *Culpables,
El baúl de los disfraces, La casa de las Chivas, Los delfines, La playa
vacía, Viaje en un trapecio.*

4. Other editions
La gran aventura. Barcelona: Editorial Millá, 1963. In "Colección Catalunya
Teatral," No. 86.
La piel del limón. Salamanca: Almar, 1980.
El corto vuello del gallo. Barcelona: Grijalbo, 1981.
In "Colección Austral." Madrid: Espasa-Calpe: *La casa de las Chivas and El
baúl de los disfraces,* no. 1529, 1973; *La noche de los cien pájaros and Los
delfines,* no. 1540, 1973; *La playa vacía and Tiempo de espadas,* No.
1598, 1975.
In "Colección Teatro." Madrid: Escelicer: *Verde esmeralda,* no. 322, 1962;
Culpables, no. 337, 1962; *El mensaje,* no. 358, 1963; *Juegos de invierno,*
no. 417, 1964; *El baúl de los disfraces,* no. 453, 1965; *Parchís Party,* no.
498, 1966; *Espejo para dos mujeres,* no. 511, 1966; *Falta de pruebas,* no.
582, 1968; *La casa de las Chivas,* no. 615, 1969; *Los delfines,* no. 638,
1969; *La playa vacía,* no. 673, 1971; *Viaje en un trapecio,* no. 684, 1971;
La noche de los cien pájaros, no. 716, 1972; *Tiempo de espadas,* no. 737,
1972; *Nueve brindis por un rey,* no. 771, 1975; *La piel del limón,* no. 783,
1976.
In Federico Carlos Sainz de Robles, ed. *Teatro español.* Madrid: Aguilar: *El
baúl de los disfraces, Teatro español, 1963–1964; La casa de las Chivas,
Teatro español, 1967–1968; Los delfines, Teatro español, 1968–1969; La
playa vacía, Teatro español, 1970–1971; La noche de los cien pájaros,
Teatro español, 1971–1972; Tiempo de espadas, Teatro español, 1972–
1973.*

SECONDARY SOURCES

ALVARO, FRANCISCO. *El espectador y la crítica.* Valladolid: Edición del
autor, 1959–1970; Madrid: Prensa Española, 1971–. This yearbook provides a synthesis of critical reaction to selected plays as well as other
information concerning theatrical productions in Spain, theater prizes,
etc. Volumes with sections devoted to individual works by Salom include those for 1960, 1964, 1965, 1967, 1969, 1970, 1972, 1974, 1976, 1978.
ANSON, LUIS MARIA. "Prólogo" to *Teatro/Jaime Salom.* Madrid: G. del Toro,
1974. Pp. 7–16. Considers Salom's mature plays to be a theater of
denunciation. Discusses *La noche de los cien pájaros* and *Tiempo de
espadas.*

ARAGONES, JUAN EMILIO. *Teatro español de posguerra.* Madrid: Publicaciones Españolas, 1971. Pp. 67–71. Brief introduction to Salom's theater with emphasis on *La casa de las Chivas.*

BLANCO Y NEGRO. "Retrato de un desconocido: Nicolás, padre de Franco," *Blanco y Negro*, October 1–7, 1980, pp. 12–16. Round table discussion reacting to Salom's *El corto vuelo del gallo.* Participants include Salom, author Emilio Romero, historian Ramón Garriga, critics Julio Trenas and Adolfo Prego, and actors María Silva and Javier Escrivá.

CAROL, JOSE. *Entre la espada y la pared. Interrogatorio a los españoles.* Barcelona: Ediciones Rondas, 1974. Pp. 255–60. Brief introduction to Salom's theater. Playwright's responses to thirty-three questions on his personal experiences and opinions.

DELGADO, JAIME. "El teatro de Jaime Salom." In *Teatro selecto de Jaime Salom.* Madrid: Escelicer, 1971. Pp. vii–lxiii. General introduction to Salom's theater and specific discussions of six plays included in anthology. Recommended. Excellent analysis of *La playa vacía* reprinted as "Prólogo" to *La playa vacía* and *Tiempo de espadas.* Madrid: Espasa-Calpe, 1975. Pp. 13–22.

GIRONELLA, JOSE MARIA and RAFAEL BORRAS BETRIU. *100 españoles y Franco.* Barcelona: Planeta, 1979. Pp. 490–502. Extensive interview exploring playwright's current attitude toward the Franco era.

HERA, ALBERTO DE LA. "*Nueve brindis para [sic] un rey* de Jaime Salom," *Primer Acto* 177 (February, 1975): 61–62. Places play in context of twentieth century historical theater. Considers Salom's farce to be trivial.

HOLT, MARION P. "Jaime Salom." In *The Contemporary Spanish Theater (1949–1972).* Boston: Twayne, 1975. Pp. 156–59. Brief but excellent introduction to subject. Discussion limited to selected plays. In English.

IZQUIERDO, JESUS. "Amor y matrimonio en la obra teatral de Jaime Salom," Master's thesis, University of Granada, 1979. Most complete source of information on Salom's theatrical activity during his student years and on his later television plays, lectures, radio series, etc. Rather superficial discussion of eighteen individual plays.

LADRA, DAVID. "Objetividad y universalidad versus realidad," *Primer Acto* 113 (October, 1969): 65–67. Review of *Los delfines.* Questions historical basis for strike. Believes that in treating the story on universal plane Salom has dehumanized his characters.

MARQUERIE, ALFREDO. *Realidad y fantasía en el teatro de Jaime Salom.* Madrid: Escelicer, 1973. Most important and extensive study of Salom to date. Includes discussions of individual plays both published and unpublished, through *Tiempo de espadas.* Groups plays according to Torres Naharro's division of "comedias a noticia" and "comedias a fantasía." General introduction on Salom's life no longer reflective of playwright's attitudes. Play analyses somewhat marred by tendency toward superficiality. Quotes extensively from other critics and from Salom's self-criticisms.

MEDINA, TICO. "Jaime Salom, el ojo y la máscara." In *De todos colores*. Barcelona: DOPESA, 1973. Pp. 33–40. Interview. Emphasis on *La noche de los cien pájaros*.

MOLERO MANGLANO, LUIS. *Teatro español contemporáneo*. Madrid: Editora Nacional, 1974. Pp. 321–35. Emphasis on *La casa de las Chivas* and *Los delfines*. Favorable analysis of the former, which he finds to be authentic drama. Criticizes latter for being dramatic essay in which characters tend to be types or symbols. Includes reviews from Barcelona papers of *El baúl de los disfraces* and *Los delfines*.

MUÑIZ, CARLOS. "*La casa de las Chivas*," *Tele/radio*, May 22–28, 1978, pp. 14–16. Review of television production. Finds that several of Salom's plays have been of timely, even prophetic, interest.

PRIMER ACTO. "Encuesta," *Primer Acto* 29–30 (December, 1961–January, 1962): 13–14. Interesting interview of playwright at beginning of theatrical career.

SAINZ DE ROBLES, FEDERICO CARLOS. "Prólogo" to *La casa de las Chivas* and *El baúl de los disfraces*. Madrid: Espasa-Calpe, 1973. Pp. 9–15. Praises Salom's theater as being profound, reflecting either realistic human problems or poetic fantasy. Considers specific two plays as representative of these basic tendencies.

———. *Teatro español*. Madrid: Aguilar, 1951–. Yearly anthology containing editor's choice of best five or six Spanish plays staged in Spain each theatrical season. Works by Salom appear in volumes for 1963–1964, 1967–1968, 1968–1969, 1970–1971, 1971–1972, 1972–1973. Each play is accompanied by the author's self-criticism along with selected play reviews.

ZATLIN-BORING, PHYLLIS. "Introducción" to Jaime Salom. *La piel del limón*. Salamanca: Almar, 1980. Pp. 11–27. Introduction to Salom's theater with special emphasis on *La piel del limón*.

———. "Jaime Salom and the Use of Doubling," *The American Hispanist*, 4, Nos. 34–35 (March–April, 1979; published in 1981), 11–14. Discussion of the doubling of actors from *El baúl de los disfraces* to *La piel del limón*.

Index